Lily Poetry Review

EDITOR-IN-CHIEF
Eileen Cleary

ASSISTANT EDITOR
Elizabeth Mercurio

ASSOCIATE EDITOR
Christine Jones

FLASH FICTION EDITORS
Mark Jednaszewski   Sarah Walker

ART EDITOR
Lisa Sullivan

VISPO EDITOR
Suzanne Mercury

WEB EDITOR
Rebecca Connors

MEDIA AND EVENTS
Frances Donovan

READERS
Susan Kay Anderson, Laura Argini, Jules Jacob, Konner Jebb,
K. T. Landon. Michelle Lynch, Gloria Monaghan, Catherine Morocco,
Tzynya Pinchback, Renuka Raghavan, Sarah Dickenson Snyder,
Mark Walsh, Anastasia Vassos, Stacey Walker, Art Zilleruelo

COVER ART, ISSUE 8
Tamara Orlowsky, *Secrets Shared*

Dear Readers,

Lily Poetry Review is pleased to present its eighth issue, signifying four years that we've been publishing beautiful art and writing. Whether you hold this journal as a contributor or reader, we are grateful to have you as part of our Lily family. We wouldn't be where we are without you, or our over 500 contributors thus far, or our dedicated and talented team of readers, layout artist, and editors.

This issue opens with Deborah Leipziger's "Vigil" so that we may bow our heads in solidarity with Ukraine. We follow by a compelling interview conducted by Art Editor Lisa Sullivan and Dzvinia Orlowsky, daughter of this edition's cover artist, Tamara Orlowsky. This artist escaped Ukraine during WWII, landing on Ellis Island in 1949. Dzvinia Orlowsky shares her insight about how her mother's paintings carry family history and stories she ultimately "can't let go of, or they, her." These paintings evoke deep emotion and connect further to what is happening today in Ukraine. This art does not speak directly to war, but as in so much great art we lionize, it speaks to the shared history and scope of our human condition, with the unique brush of an individual's perception. It cannot help but be particular to its homeland, as well as universal. It is our pleasure to introduce you to the incredible Tamara Orlowsky, and we hope you will long remember her work.

This issue celebrates the bridge of parents and their adult children in other ways as well. Max Heinegg's "Father's Day" for his father and Sarah Kilgallon's visual art created to honor her mother's lifelong avocation in poetry are two examples. Kilgallon's mother recently succumbed to Alzheimer's Disease, and her poem, embedded in her daughter Sarah's art is her posthumous debut.

It's true that our minds are on war. Corine Topal writes, "after the war the world is small again." As we await the day there is no war, we also focus on what Phoebe Reeves describes as "blooms of paper yellow and a quiet, private pink" and Steven Cramer's "particles light-years apart, how they still touch." We focus on what unites us, sustains us, even what transports us. We cannot have an actual astral escape such as the delightful one provided to Gladys Kravitz in Evelyn Enfield's debut poem, but perhaps we can be transported by all of this art, be it word or image.

The confluences of conflict and resilience, sorrow and celebration resonate throughout the issue with its poetry, art, visual poetry, and flash fiction. We hope this allows you an opportunity to contemplate and reflect. As Steven Ostrowski's "The Aging Process" states in its opening, "It's the noticing."

We invite you to notice as you read and reread.

Sincerely,

Eileen Cleary. Christine Jones. Elizabeth Mercurio.

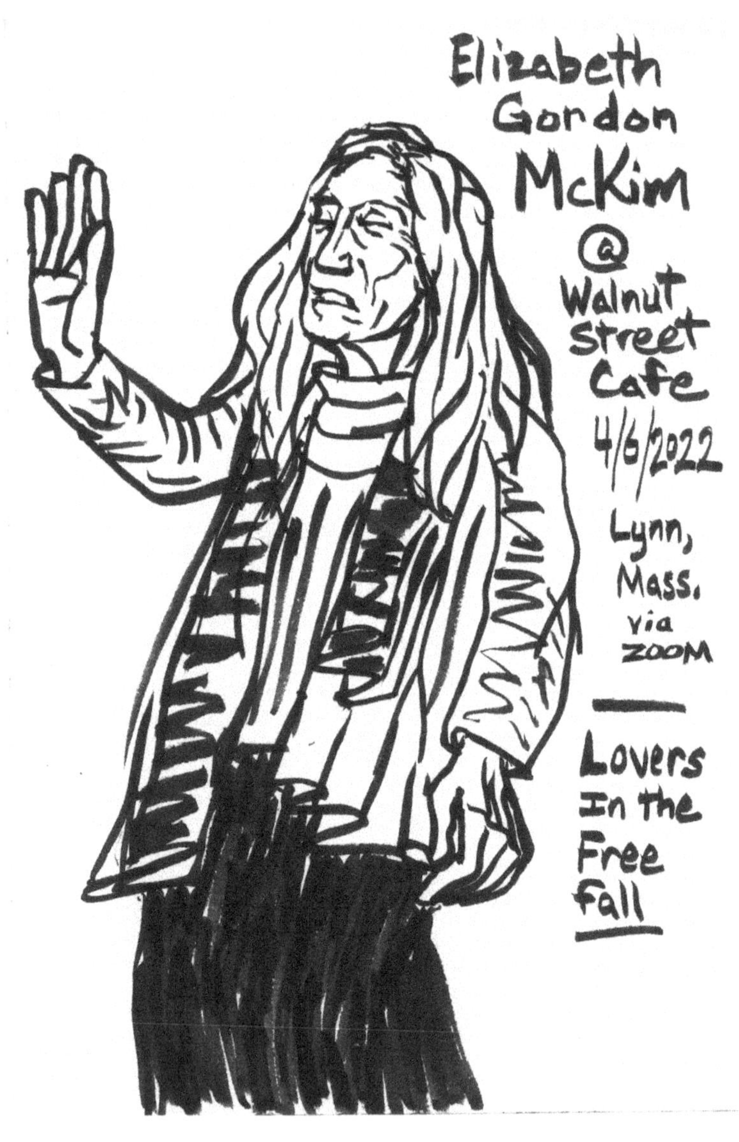

drawing by Peter Urkowitz

iv

ELIZABETH GORDON MCKIM

Directions

Hold
It. Warm it
With your own
Life. Listen
To its near and far
Pulse its sounds
Its messages.
Find out where it is born
The year the time
And who was there
And why. Find out the nature
Of its fear. What cave
Or cliff or curve
Of tide has touched
You tended you
Mended
You. Find out what
You can know
Of parents
What song or language
You were taught
And if you have a friend, a lullaby
To help you wake and dream
What scars and marks
Distinguish
You and if you have a friend
An enemy what surface
Opens to the air, what
Inside heart is hiding there, and learn
The way you live and breathe
And how you move upon
This earth

CONTENTS

DEBORAH LEIPZIGER

Vigil

> For the Ukraine

The open window, the birds, the rain,
all stand sentry.

May they linger.

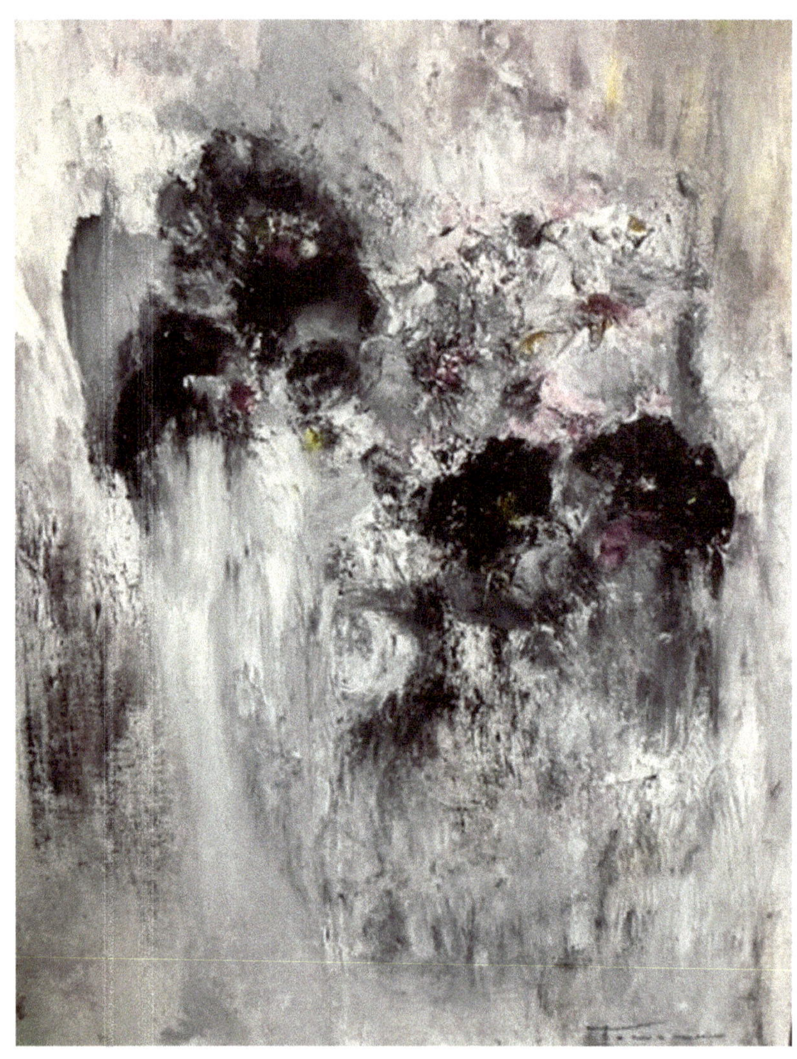

Pocket of Wildflowers

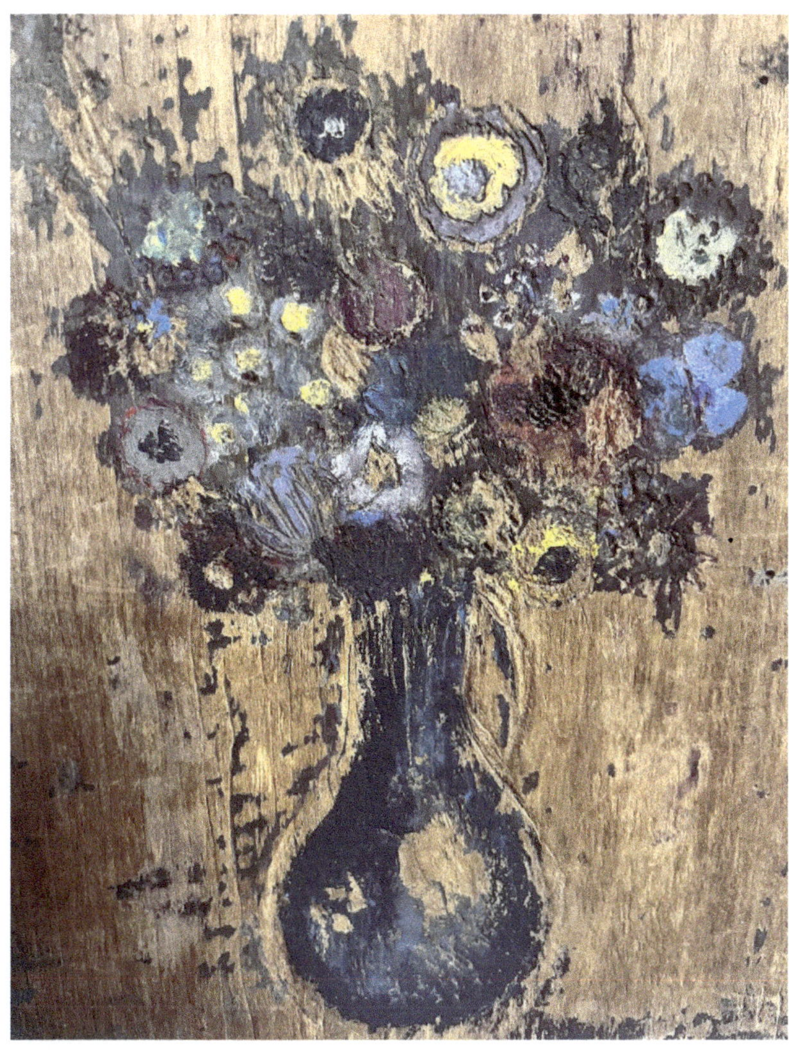

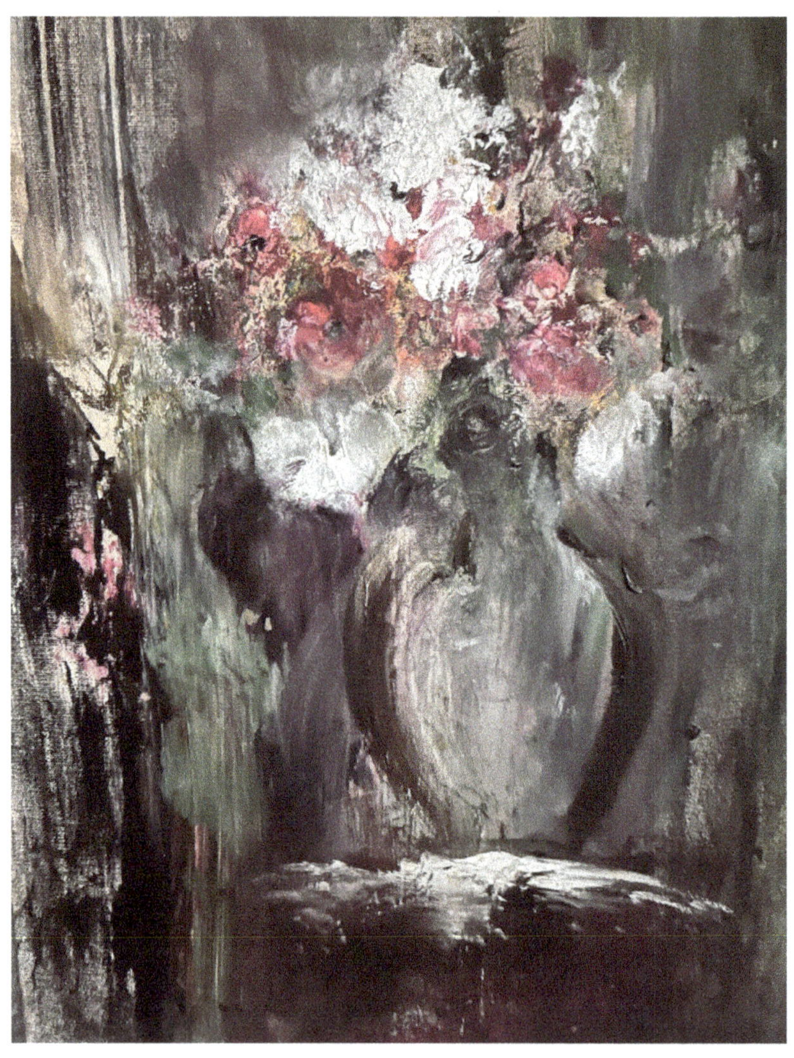

TAMARA ORLOWSKY · **Moonflower**

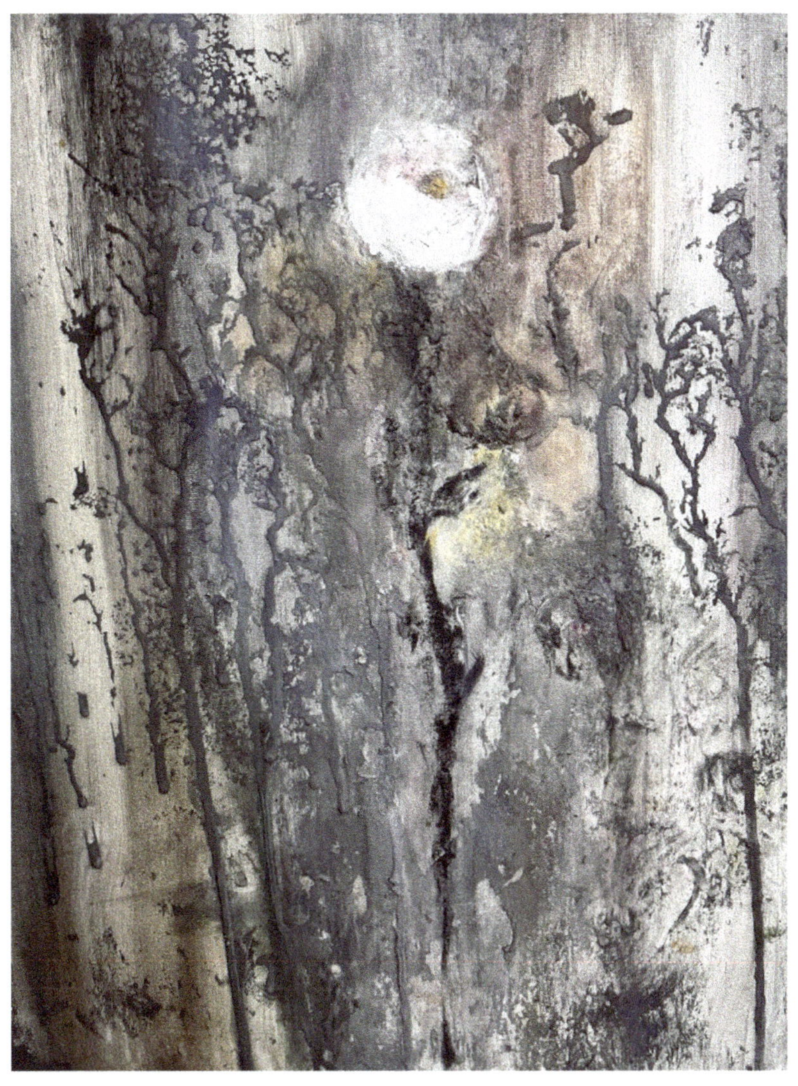

  Breaking Silence

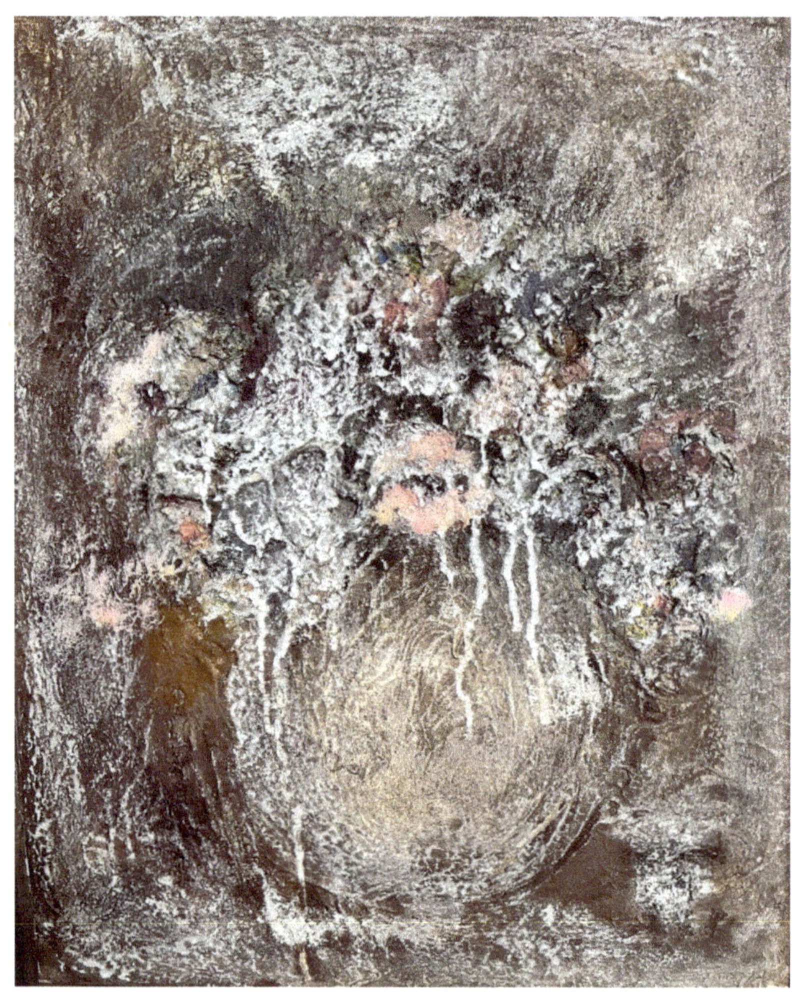

Meadow's End

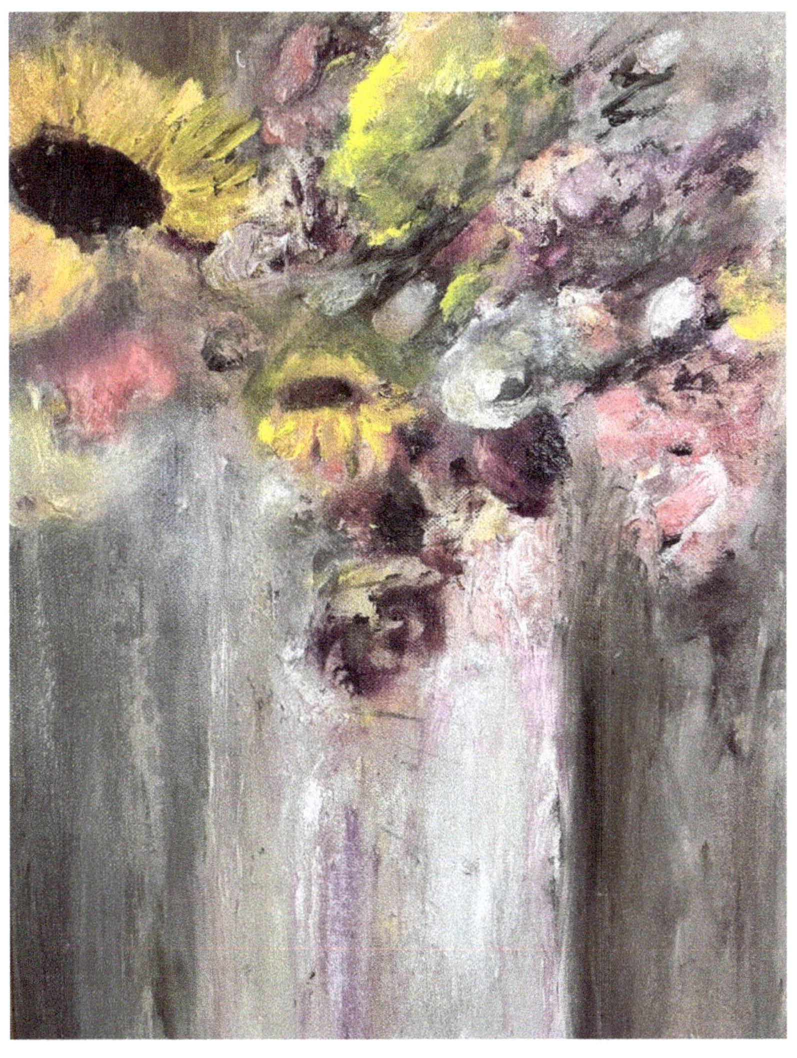

Murau, Austria, 1944. *The biggest sorrow for me on my wedding day—for which I had dreamt and waited so long—was that it would be without flowers. While Mirko tended to more formal matters, I ran like a mad woman to the back of the church to pick or steal at least one flower. It was the beginning of March when all of nature's beauty still lay in the mountains. But I found my good fortune and happiness, its partner, by the gate near the back church door—a few pink and yellow wildflowers that bloomed early as if to show themselves before the earth was taken over with human-seeded flowers.*

(From Tamara Orlowsky's journal, translated by her daughter, Dzvinia Orlowsky)

Tamara Orlowsky (née Bonczuk) was born on February 11, 1920, in Zhmerynka, Southwestern Ukraine. She recalled her father hiding in a neighbor's armoire to avoid being shot by Bolshevik soldiers. And how, as a young woman, she hid in the basement, blocking her ears to muffle the cries of Jewish families dragged into the streets by Nazis. At the tail end of WWII, escaping Nazis and Stalin's communist forces, Tamara, her husband, Miroslaus (Mirko), and her parents fled Ukraine via Austria. They arrived on Ellis Island in 1949.

Tamara began painting in her 50s. She often worked at night, the hours when she was most creative. Contrasting or complementary color tonalities and Impressionistic brush strokes expressed the essence of a subject rather than the exact reproduction of it. Self-taught, she exhibited in group and solo shows throughout Ohio, New York, and Massachusetts but favored sharing her work in her studio. Mystical flowers gathered into vanishing or nonexistent vases remained her one subject throughout her life. She died peacefully in Scituate, Massachusetts on August 30, 2007.

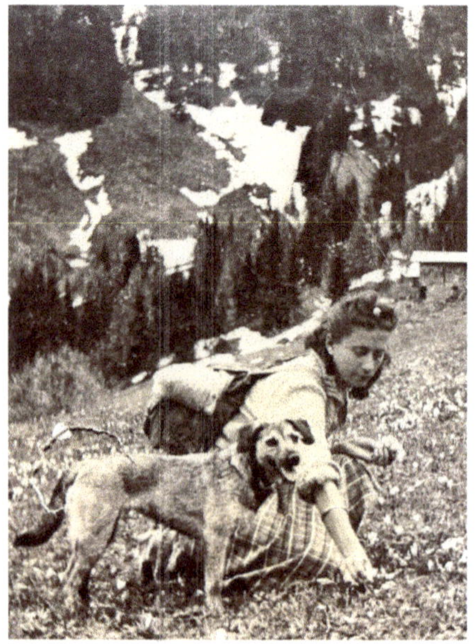

I think my paintings give people the feeling that they are looking through a window on a rainy day.

Tamara Orlowsky
2/11/1920 - 8/30/2007

8

Interview with Dzvinia Orlowsky, daughter of Ukrainian Featured Artist, Tamara Orlowsky

Lisa Sullivan: Thank you, Dzvinia, for spending some time with us today to talk about your mother's exquisite paintings. I'd like to start off by asking whether your mom painted her flower studies from nature, still life, or her mind's eye?

Dzvinia Orlowsky: Thank you, Lisa. It's my great pleasure.

My mother painted mostly from her mind's eye—life experiences that left an impression on her. But "from nature" also. In her earliest paintings, when we lived in Ohio, she experimented with wood-working tools carving floral textures into weathered barn wood salvaged from collapsed barns which were then highlighted with oil paints. To create texture in her later canvas pieces, she sometimes used dried, pressed flower petals, twigs, glue, and always thick, expressive, brushstrokes.

Tamara never painted from "still life." Misinterpreting the genre, she tended to call a finished piece her "still alive."

LS: Out of curiosity, do you know what your mom's favorite flower was? And how about your favorite flower?

DO: Tamara's favorite flowers were wild violets. Loosely gathered, small bouquets of them filled the rooms of our home. She also adored silk millinery violets that she pinned on the front tie of her empire-waist dresses. My sister, Maria, and her daughter, Tessa, and my daughter, Raisa, and I were each gifted with a bunch which we, too, pinned to our best dresses or later, to our college backpacks. I still have my lovely bouquet, and I keep a bottle of violet-scented eau de toilette on my bedroom dresser to remind me of her.

My favorite flower would have to be Lily of the Valley, or Lily of the Alley, as a young Raisa used to call (and invent songs about) them. They're a bountiful flower, symbolically optimistic, and often paired with violets.

LS: Please tell us about Tamara's studio. What was the environment like?

DO: Her primary studio was a room in her in-law apartment in my sister's house. It was dark, filled with raw, barn wood furniture my mother brought with her from Ohio. A staticky FM radio played classical music while she worked. She painted on a wooden easel or a center café table which when not in use was draped with a scarf-like tapestry or an old fishing net. She had grown to love the ocean. Her studio was decorated with a few finished paintings, some family memorabilia, but mostly pieces of driftwood and stones she collected from her walks on the beach. The main source of light came from three windows overlooking her garden, accented with weathered bird houses.

LS: I know your mom was self-taught and her work has many qualities of 19th-century Impressionism. Are you aware of any Impressionist painters or other artists she admired or was influenced by?

DO: My mother collected postcards of paintings that moved her. Included among those were paintings by Monet, Van Gogh, Renoir, and Pissarro. She found kinship with their thick, textured brushstrokes, and impression over clear form greatly appealed to her.

LS: One of the features of your mom's paintings that I find highly evocative is the suggestion of the vases. Did she ever share her thoughts on that with you?

DO: Yes, she basically didn't like painting vases, so she did her best to minimize their presence. Her flowers characteristically emerge out of the background. Rather than containing them, the vase, or suggestion of a vase, is there primarily to ground them in the foreground. Often, she omitted vases altogether.

Father Yaroslav Nalysnyk, pastor of the Ukrainian Catholic Church in Jamaica Plain, Massachusetts, to which she belonged, after attending one of her exhibits, noted it was particularly intriguing that her flowers never seemed to touch the ground.

LS: As many of our readers may know, you are a highly published, award-winning poet. Have you ever written ekphrastically about your mom's paintings? If not, is it something you may consider?

DO: Thank you, Lisa. I've only written one ekphrastic poem based on a painting by Tamara. It's called "Glue Wind" from my most recent book, Bad Harvest. The poem describes a painting depicting a pair of swirling snow funnels created with Elmer's Glue. The speaker must squint hard to find the flowers. She momentarily questions her need to always see things through her mother's eyes, realizing like the wind, her paintings carry family history and stories she ultimately can't let go of, or they, her.

And I have your gorgeous sonnet, Lisa, "Oil Painting, Upstairs (Tamara)" which you gifted me in 2017 which hangs framed in my study. So now there are two Ekphrastic Tamara poems! Maybe one day, there will be more.

LS: Your mom stated, "I think my paintings give people the feeling that they are looking through a window on a rainy day." Indeed! Can you elaborate on what her thought process may have been regarding that statement?

DO: Flowers embodied the representation of her deepest life experiences both joyful and sad. The flowers seen through the rainy window perhaps represent the joy that despite troubling times, if you look carefully enough, can always be found.

As she grew older and more reluctant or unable to verbalize her feelings about her past, I believe these flowers, collectively, became a subconscious self-portrait. The rainy-day metaphor was replaced by her term: "crying flowers"—which for her, better expressed the feelings she wanted to get across.

LS: The cover of this issue of *Lily Poetry Review* is blessed with your mom's haunting painting, "Moonflower." When choosing this cover art, it brought to mind the current, devastating state of your mom's native Ukraine due to Russia's cruel, unprovoked invasion, and the Ukrainian people's valiant response (symbolized by the hopeful "moonflower" rising above, or growing out of, the darkness). Do you recall whether any of your mom's paintings were influenced by her time in Ukraine?

DO: I believe in some way they all are. Even though she painted flowers inspired by her life in America, I feel it was with a constant reflecting, looking back.

I recall one larger, more abstract painting that gave the impression of a hefty grid superimposed on what appeared to be crushed flowers. She told me it represented tank treads destroying a meadow.

LS: Are your mother's paintings available for exhibition? If any of our readers wish to connect with you regarding Tamara's work, could you please share your contact information here?

DO: Most of Tamara's paintings are either in my home or Maria's, though a number were sold at exhibits or gifted to close friends and unfortunately, over time, lost track of. They are available for exhibition, and anyone wishing to contact me regarding that possibility or her paintings in general can do so through email, messenger, or my website: www.dzviniaorlowsky.com. I'd love to hear from you!

LS: Thank you again for sharing your mom's gorgeous, moving paintings with us. I'd like to close by asking a difficult question— which of your mom's paintings is your favorite and what does it symbolize to you?

DO: Thank you Lisa for featuring Tamara's paintings in Lily Poetry Review and for your thoughtful, perceptive questions. I really appreciate your making time to do so.

Because my mother's paintings reflect such a wide range of moods and emotions, it's difficult to choose one over the other. In her paintings, I see happiness, awe, desire, but I also see sadness, distress, bewilderment. I would like to say my favorite is any one of her paintings that represents happiness. I want to remember her as happy.

Having said that, however, "Winter's Flowers" is probably a favorite. I love the deep color palette and because, like two others that hang next to it, "Moonflower" and "Breaking Silence," the painting speaks to me about survivorship. A first snowfall covers the flowers—the "weeping" field of white on the left threatens to erase them—but they remain present, nonetheless. Unlike snowdrops which suggest innocence and renewal, these flowers suggest loss. Several are rendered a deep, blood red, while others appear white. Perhaps they are slowly becoming one with the snow, but they haven't forfeited their beauty.

LINDAANN LOSCHIAVO

Hazards of New Fortune

I. Fortune

"Every disadvantage has its advantage."   — *Ukrainian proverb*

"Кожен недолік має свою перевагу."   — *Russian translation*

They quit the Ukraine for America, sacred place of new beginnings. Rescuing a forsaken candy shop with workman's grit, their first business rooted, flourished, blossomed. Wrap-around windows shed sunlight on Slavic menus, neatly folded by the oldest daughter. A famous East Village poet dined here often, a Pied Piper who lured others. Yet waiting tables, washing dishes felt lowly as a casual betrayal even as New York repainted their family portrait in greenbacks and gold. At closing time, each customer was tumbled out, like a salt shaker, which magically refilled, then emptied out again. Full bellies fast-friended the cash register. Optimized aliveness.

> daily chores
> the weight of
> waiting

II. New

“Flies will not land on a boiling pot.”   *— Ukrainian proverb*

“На киплячий казан мухи не сідають.Eage.”   *— Russian translation*

New profits ballooned into a real estate portfolio, deeds fingered like dominos. The restaurateurs sipped life lazily through a straw of wealth, the holy liturgy of labor now handed off to helpers. After customers left, the family supped together on smoked kielbasa, challah bread, boiled potatoes, picking the diced carrots from the borscht to eat one at a time like golden pills — as if to protect themselves from what would come.

      corner diner
      the ceiling fan
      idly turns

III. Of

"The earth will cover a doctor's mistakes."   *— Ukrainian proverb*

"Земля закроет ошибки врача."   *— Russian translation*

Of a day unlike the rest. Of a sky cutting itself open, bleeding dawn's red readiness. Of an unbearable pressure. Of air spawning pearls of sweat. Of a terror gliding through squares of daylight on the bedroom floor. Of struggling to sit up, watching blankets rise as if winged. Of final utterings unheard from a fifty-year-old mouth. Of wondering why a black umbrella blows open under his eyelids at a wild storm king's command. Of inner momentum shorted out.

     silent cue
     stilling life's hum
     last breath

* Note: The East Village (NYC) gas explosion happened on
Thursday, March 26, 2015.

MAHMOUD EL-MARDI

Windows of the Middle East and North Africa

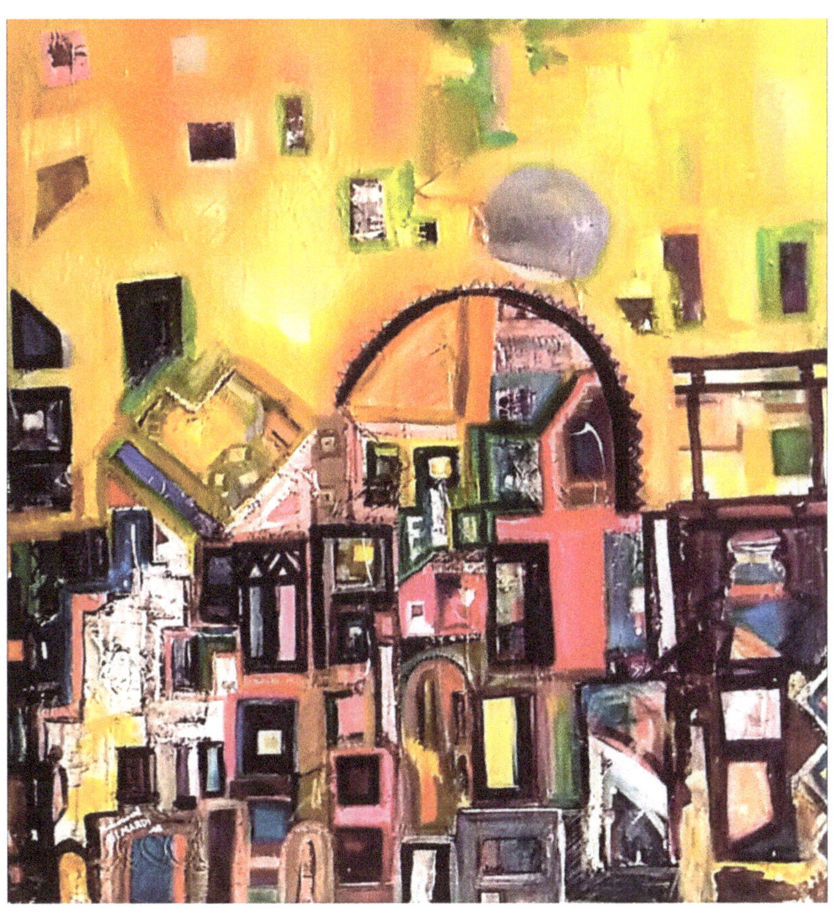

JANICE D. SODERLING

Full Moon Over Athens

Deep underground the broken relics rest.
A fractured frieze or clasp, a carved bone flute.
Sometimes the finest, sometimes second best;
a dented shield or heart, a stringless lute.

A fractured clasp or word, or champagne flute.
They were, these lovers, skilled at breaking things,
Her dented heart, his shield, a stiff-necked lute.
They warred with the civility of kings.

They were, these lovers, skilled at breaking things:
vows, promises and treaties. And they waged
their love with the civility of kings.
Love's buried now, and both of them have aged.

Now promises, entreaties, wars they waged
seem less than finest—hardly second-best.
All buried now. Dear God, so fast we've aged.
Deep underground, the broken relics rest.

KALI LIGHTFOOT

Before there were weather forecasts,

we humans looked for mares' tail
clouds, and mackerel skies—

noted wax and wane of rheumatiz,
listened for peepers

and katydids, watched
cumulus stack up or drift.

We gazed without thoughts of
intellicasting, stalled pressure

systems, or radar towers.
We ambled, foraged and tended

flocks under whimsical clouds.
We lived in the unmapped paths

of hurricanes that arrived unnamed.
We squinted after nightfall

into darkness, sniffing the wind.

MARTHA MCCOLLOUGH

Disputed territories

the night massive   light-winged

      a vacancy   carried on the air

lantern
little device
of beauty

behind a wall pocked with shell holes

      the cards keep my creepy secrets—

minor romance
with death   desire's
embarrassments—

between a pack of cards

        and pack of wolves

choose wolves-at-a-distance
howling with a ruined piano
as the tanks approach

pinwheel of sparks

      the velocity   and the sensation

ELLEN AUSTIN-LI

Mountain Song for My Nephew

What matter if I live it all once more?
                              -W.B. Yeats

Four years now. The canvas a pasture
with this grazing horse before he breaks
into a gallop, mane flying, some wings, such joy
to be pounding the earth with hooves.
It's not fair, you being gone. You shouldn't be

the body absent the stream. I wake every day
and think my small thoughts about what I need
to weed from the garden, to dust in the house,
the poem I must write to fix you
on the page. It's not minor I've forgotten

your eyes. Were they hazel or blue? The minor
key sounds like loss, your tattoos no longer
sharp, the notes floating on this bar of abstraction
in feathered wisps. The song coils the ridge,
and you, the peak profiled against the sky.

SHELEEN MCELHINNEY

The Blue Bird

All the poets are talking about winter. The diamond crusted collars

of snow draped around the necks of trees, the branches so laden they bow

to the street. Lakes frozen to still mirrors against the sky, it's reflection

unmoved. They talk about lifting their faces, opening their mouths

in the dark just to see their own breath reach the stars. But I can't stop

thinking about the summer, years ago, when I bought a pale blue

bird and palmed it into a cage. It's miniature heart chittering under my thumb,

under the milk white down of its chest, the frantic flutter of wings,

it's dander dancing in golden slices of light. Wild birds from the window

taunting it with their infinite expanse of sky, how cold I was then.

SUSAN GRIMM

When I woke up into my head

When I woke up into my head   there was so much to agree to
infinite plain   wildebeest   what kind of weather is this

I knew the world with its clumps and stains   but I had trouble
with my part   I was leaking   ungelled   the thing

contained telescope-broken   and cups all over the place
no manual for shipwrecks   but electrode sites inked

onto my scalp   without choice   I took form
as a cloud   without underwear   in other news   slowness

bubble-topped dread   in a geriatric cabinet   scoured out
all the things I must deliver   spoon-stirred or by pontoon

 Facing It Series Mixed Media

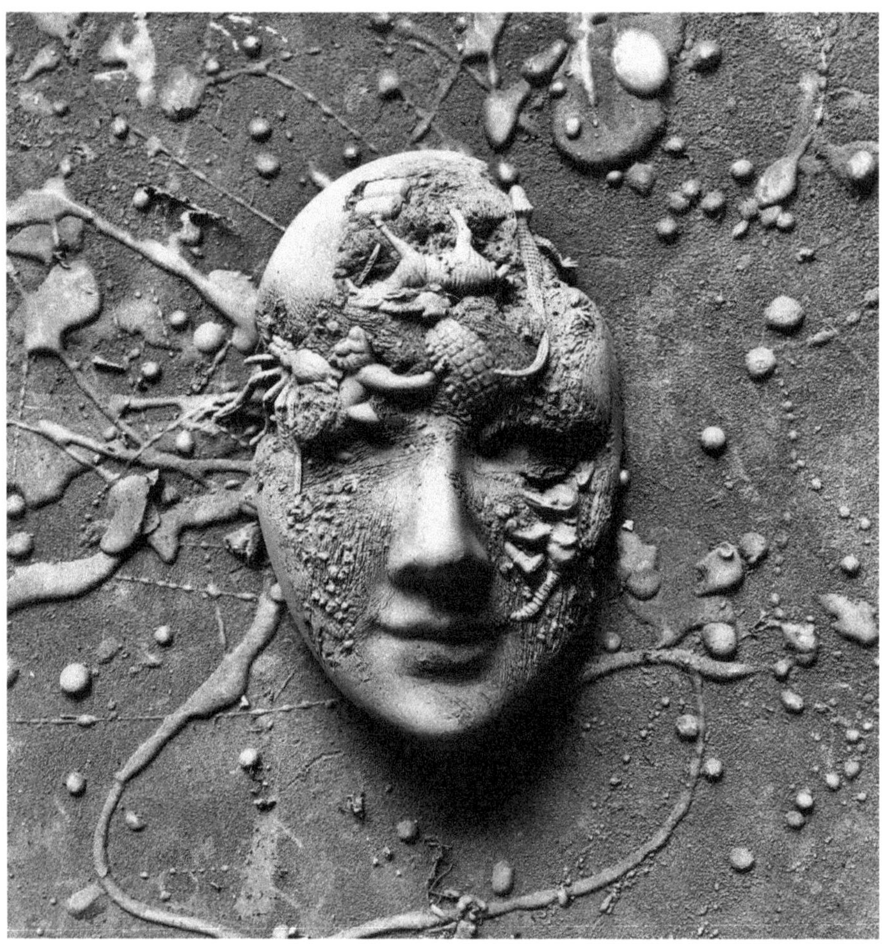

MAX HEINEGG

Elegy

—For Po

In the manner of December
trees that know they will again
be rain's familiar, not bound by
the climbing ice. The heart knows
that it is branch as well
as flower, offering into darkness
small gift for the ceremony.
If the branch holds tightly,
it is because it knows winter
reaches for the roots, & life strains
to extend in shadow. Even fallen,
the branch remembers flower. So,
love calls for you like a father,
to be sure you are there.

MAX HEINEGG

Father's Day 2021

In the weeks after my father dies,
I see him everywhere alive.

The man that left me, mistaken
for gone-out-walking white haired men

who laze on benches, craning forward
to nose their menus, fretting orders—

who stand to read the news aghast
and lean into their arguments,

riveted to invisible worlds.
I'm assured by every echo of

that voice. I follow wherever
I can hear it, into the hearsay

of the leaves, into my limited
future, into philippics of wind,

into a too-late eulogy,
as if the half a century

I was given to learn the secrets
my father guards were insufficient

to see his failures truthfully.
Even as I dream I hold his body,

(his eyes diving out of his mind,
my arms stronger for the dread)

is gone. The form no longer
an actor, or the world a stage for

an audience that does not want to be
here. I would give anything to leave.

STEVEN CRAMER

Coulomb's Law

Because the atoms that make your fingers
repel the atoms that make mine,
when touching, we don't touch—
our mutual repulsions saving us
from blowing up; but isn't this a comfort
cold as the marbles orbiting a softball,
the planetary prototype *Our Friend the Atom*
got all wrong? Given Quantum Entanglement—
particles light-years apart keep in touch,
their spooky relations riling even Einstein—
maybe love's best left subatomic.
Meanwhile, we wander about heedless,
me tricked into thinking I'm me and you
you. Claw out the brain pan, and the soul
in there, or call it what you will, is pure wetware.
Who's that painter who made lovemaking
look like hunks of colliding meat? Man, it was sick:
pigment lathered up into a froth of flesh.
Bacon—that's him; *pig* brought his bad name back.
"Define touch," some have said, but really—
more you push, the harder the pushback.
Particularly speaking, aren't we all
over the place? In the beautiful *Bright Star,*
the English Romantic I love best raps twice
on a wall to call his beloved, and the twin taps
she sends back touch his lips like a kiss.

STEVEN CRAMER

"A Word Made Flesh"

–Franklin #1714; Johnson #1651

1
The Garden State I grew up in was no
Arboretum, let alone Eden. Trees said

tree to me, and I still can't tell an elm
from an oak or gray from paper birch.

Searching *whin,* I get *furze,* which links
to *gorse:* three names name one shrub's

prickly, trifoliate leaves and showy petals
rooted in the moorlands of Old Norse.

2
Maybe she played the game we played:
say, and say and say, one word—*alligator,*

say—until the olive-brown Floridian fades
to its syllables, wordless as the worm, lank

and pink, she dreamt into her winter room
then shrank from: a swelling, fluent snake.

3 *This Loved Philology*
Dated to her late reticence, "A Word
made Flesh is seldom" makes me say

what she once said all men say to her—
what—but its parting line, paraphrased:

"this beloved love of language"—lovely
tautology!—tells poetry's twice-told tale:

all words stem from origins unknown.

STEVEN CRAMER

How the Mail Used to Feel

Rapture's off-rhyme with *torture.*
Luckily, a ruby or two, like ransom
paid, brightened the junkpile of flat whites.
A couple bills or fliers still pitch their static
through the slot, like plucked sprigs of thyme.
Paper cuts welcome, long as the words draw blood.
Maybe that's why I'm haplessly rereading *Gatsby*
without the pocket handkerchief, its scent
redolent of the stripes, scrolls, and coral plaids
Jay piles like bricks in stacks a dozen high, all
the while *they're beautiful shirts,* sobs Daisy. . .
Maybe I've discovered why I go for movies
instead of plays: no dénouement when a door
sticks; no heart attack collapsing the fourth wall.
Life just sometimes lasts a lifetime, its school
uniform all itches. We usually still sit still, and care.
For a while I was headed for the exits myself,
then got ahead of me and saw who I'd become
if I became history to everybody else,
my neighbor whose weeding looks like praying
excluded. I wish I'd stop seeing people
as getaways from the bank that robbed them.
For now, let me persist, blesséd, and not take
walks anymore with my long-gone friend I loved
along the yellow-strewn sidewalk under Linnaean's
gingko after fall gingko, the only tree I know
that loses all its leaves in a single day.

ANNIE STENZEL

Blumenfenster

I sit before an object that lays claim to the word, *window*, and pretend
three vases, filled to the brim with flowers, once inspired my half-blind
great-uncle to reach for rose madder, Venetian red, yellow primrose
instead of the green and thundercloud grey that made most
of his other images a guarantee of sadness, deep and long.

NANCY WHITE

Carpenter

image: in a stand of trees
a shanty nailed up
off the ground

cobbled together
rusty nails a crate with a cup
tin box two candles

what tool for
capture for lasting what
place we could belong in

or to a house in trees
not structure but idea
about structure the made

cobbling together will
not fail us not rot not fall not
ladder let us fall

it is so much to ask a
small barely weatherproof
shelter in the trees

CARINE TOPAL

Threadbare, We Are Homesick

After the war the world is small again. Enough has survived to start a country. For miles, as far as the eye takes you, towns hardly alive tilt on the sand. Stopped trains wait for something to move them. The air is thick with worry. I search for a quartet in the town of my people but find no one but a desperate boy pointing to my cello, which I hold onto, belly-down. It is my father as a boy. Who knows how, in the half-lit morning hours, people see what they long for? In this shadow world there is no father, just the slight weight of his memory, the human moan of my cello, the ghostly groan seeking four chairs for a chamber, a night-song to hold me alone in this new republic. I am homesick, I do not know where home is. But a faraway music holds my attention: the adagio I played years ago while Father sat for hours in his chair and hummed. An impressive audience, enough to fill the town, sits atop the moving trains, fanning themselves with their top hats and berets. On cue we open with an effortless *adagio* for strings whose middle-passage initiates a slight dynamic change to *andante*. Now listeners hold their hats. Hours pass but they do not stir, until dusk, with the roused *allegretto*, when they animate as though suddenly wound up, throwing carnations, shouting bravos. My father sits beside me playing his violin. We play on, losing ourselves in the dry earth. We are part of the earth's décor, our swaying bodies polished in the next sun, our tears pooling at the small scratch of our wood. We have no worries. Penniless, not broken, we move from town to town, appearing suddenly out of the dust. The same trains stand on their tracks. The same people wait as if to preserve the heartbeat. Ah, Mozart, man of loose buttons, the flustered nerve of the world taking up most of the sky. *Con affeto.*

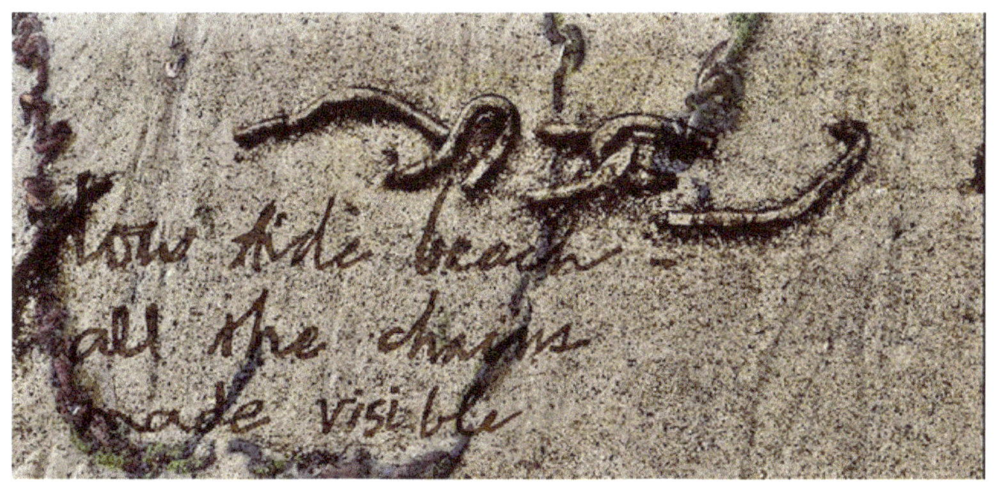
low tide beach
all the chains
made visible

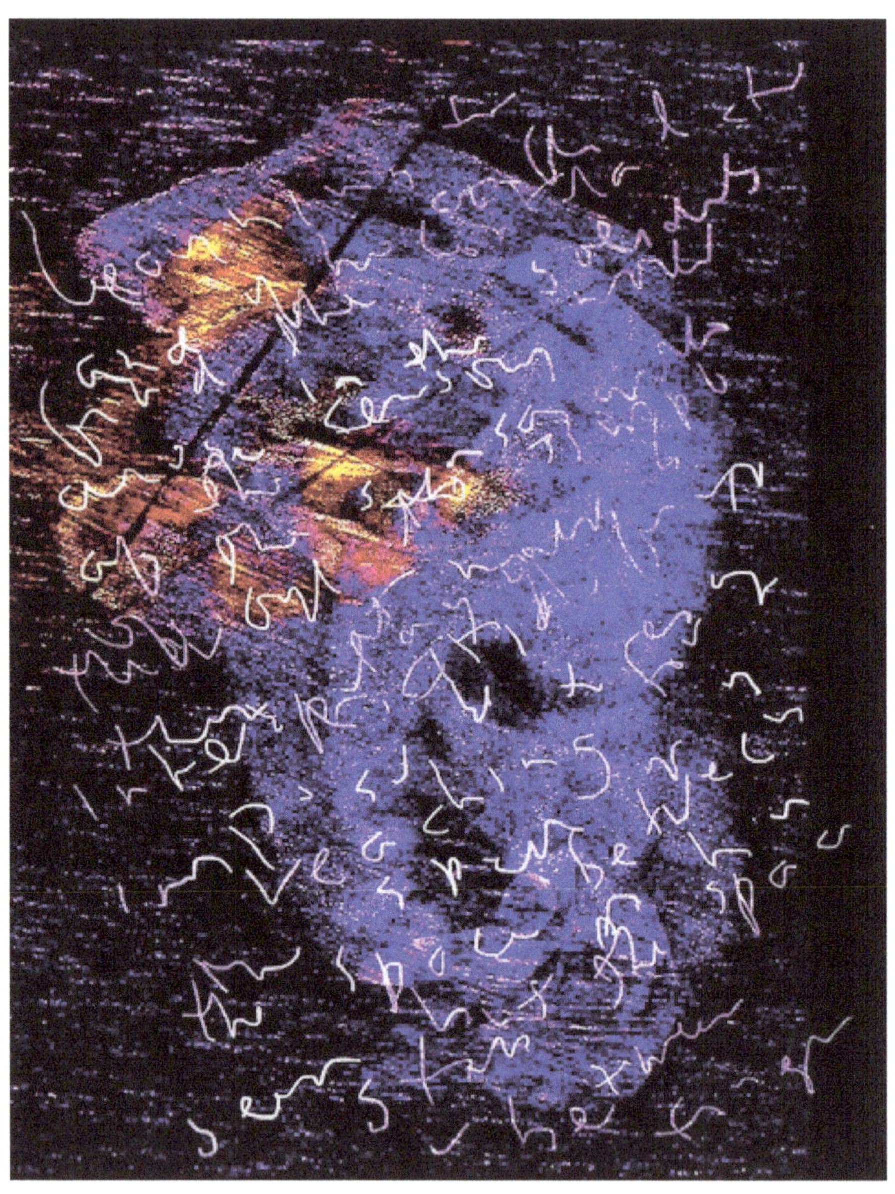

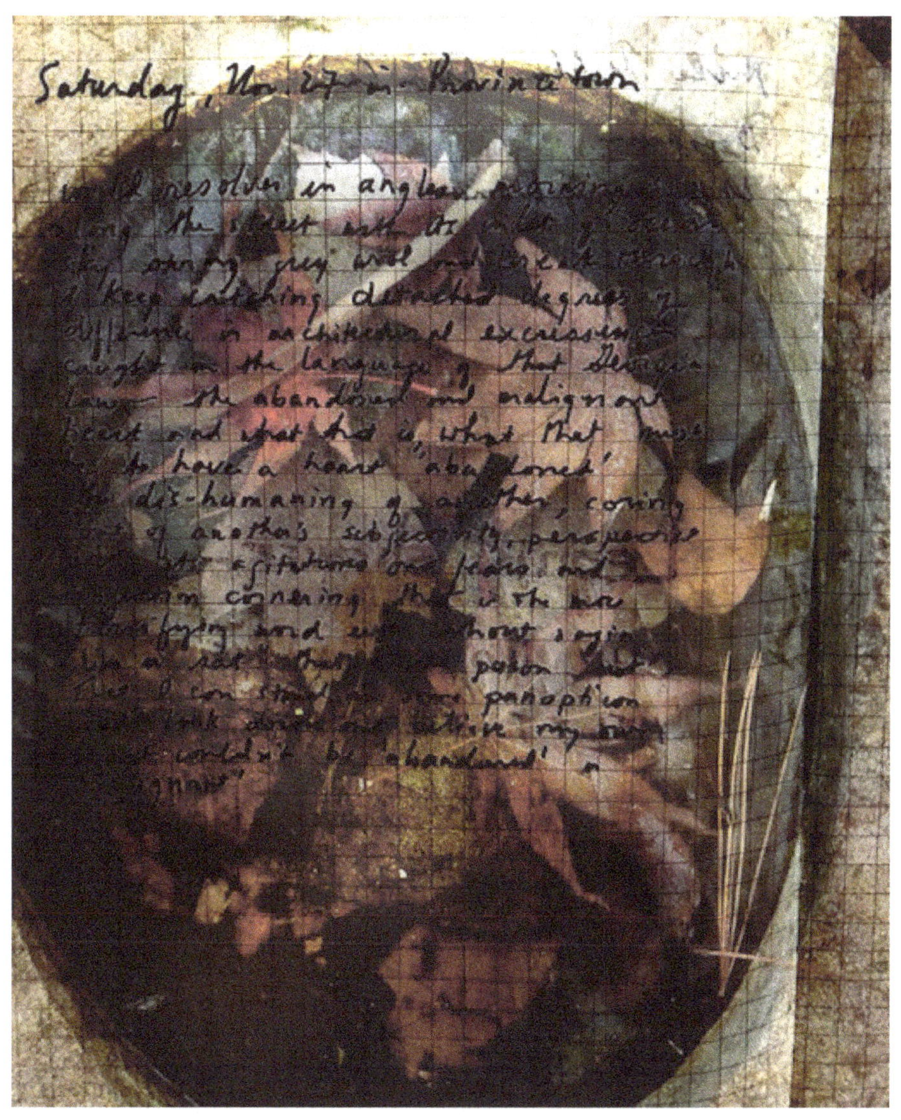

LAUREL BENJAMIN

Visionary

We had the night sky
as my brother snuck out
and five minutes later, I followed

to avoid our parent's radar.
What did we fear—
father's analysis, the Rorscharch blots

mother's card catalogue schedule
and neatly buttoned shirtwaist dresses
slipping us into slots?

My brother saw circles, snails, rotating wheels.
He traced them with his index finger,
his cornea containing a telescope.

Brother, did the stars cast a spell,
you who spent years in special schools
reversing letters in words?

He mapped constellations
while I played hangman
in the back row of geometry.

On a Sierra Club trip we lay our bones
against granite boulders
as the leader introduced the Western sky

where light beams
fell to earth.
Star upon star.

If we stayed long enough, a parade
of orange and purple,
a swatch of cool green

like courage
that we'd need
after the stars faded.

LAUREL BENJAMIN

While She Blotted Her Lipstick

I wish my mother had been more precise like the photos in her head
of her mother and the brownstone. Or had turned her pocketbook inside out

on the mosaic coffee table, ingredients like foam from the sea, murky then clear.
Or in a major key she had praised my Telemann solo but that would have

broken me. On my own, I learned to scow through what could be had cheap,
and in garrulous form ignored the absolute, but I could not hear the cry of a gull

as it threw its breast forward, or see the lunge of a scorpion. I wish she had ceased fire
the missiles she couldn't resist so I could rest my hand in hers

before the stroke, not after.

DAVID P. MILLER

Her Parents' House

golden shovel, after James Wright

For Sale lawn-staked, suddenly.

Finished winnowing, she and I.

No further prelude left to realize.

One year of sorting memory comes to that.

No *maybe* for his rafts of tools, no *if*

for their grandfather clock. She and I

will retain her family plot, stepped

above the harbor. Our last way out.

Goodbye juice glasses. No more of

end tables. Goodbye porch niche, my

chassis in the rocker's creaking body.

Ever less entangled, this we call *I*.

Pared to our one roof. What else would

freshen our autumns? We'll break

ground again above the harbor. Fade into

a houseless blossom.

JULIA LISELLA

Just Outside the Garden, the Irises

Just outside the garden, or where the garden used to be,
where I'd stand quietly watching my father
re-measure and cordon off our plot each spring
holding the ends of the sprung measuring tape for him,
or pouring the seeds from their crisp packet
(some seeds like an infant's gold earring
spilling too quickly from my small palm,
some seeds flat like the bugs we found
in the kitchen drawer, easy to lay down in the tracks.)
the irises my sister planted after my father could no longer work the ground
spread blue and violet across the fence between the Cape Cods.
Though thick-stemmed, they are easy to clip
and I'm dizzy with the spread they make in my fist now,
their petals sturdy and flush. I carry them into the house
once filled with the life of my parents, their tender
negotiations: what they would have to eat,
which greens from the garden they'd steam.
I place the vase on my mother's bureau.
In her centenarian sleep-wake-sleep
I think she sees them, or sees my father.
I leave her conversing with the air.

REBECCA RESSL

Body Blushed Into

On weaning day,
Mama became
a crow foot cauldron hung
for dinner, her amethyst pocket
filled with herb gardens,
pollen and thorn.

Sundusted cicada shells
crusted her insides.
Half blood. Half sap.
Nature, nurture, nourish,
it isn't all symbiotic in the end.

She watched her son grow into
robin blue egg mornings
and full moon nights,
while her body blushed into
a bruised shadow of a line,
a trick of the light.

STEVEN OSTROWSKI

The Aging Process

It's the noticing. It's the electric angles and magnetic turns the sun
takes all day so your pixels can spark. It's touching your lover again,
astonished for the thousandth time, renewed like authentic shyness. It's
another redemption story unfolding in the garden, tolled by flowerbells
in shadowless sun. It's a song about the pleasure-guilty foretaste of
innocence and remembering what you expected of tomorrow and
then forgot until now. It's the rubbing of your eyes in the morning
and at evening the sweet humility of lowering your knees to the floor,
belief and unbelief truced and twined with prayerlike acceptance. It's
the kids and the kids' kids lining up for kisses. It's that just today you
noticed there's a wooden house with a wide porch set way back in the
woods, all weedy, overgrown, decrepit, wayward, noble, gorgeous.
It's wondering why, all these years as you drove this curling green
undulation of a road, your favorite road on earth, that that house was
always there and you never noticed it. It's the noticing now.

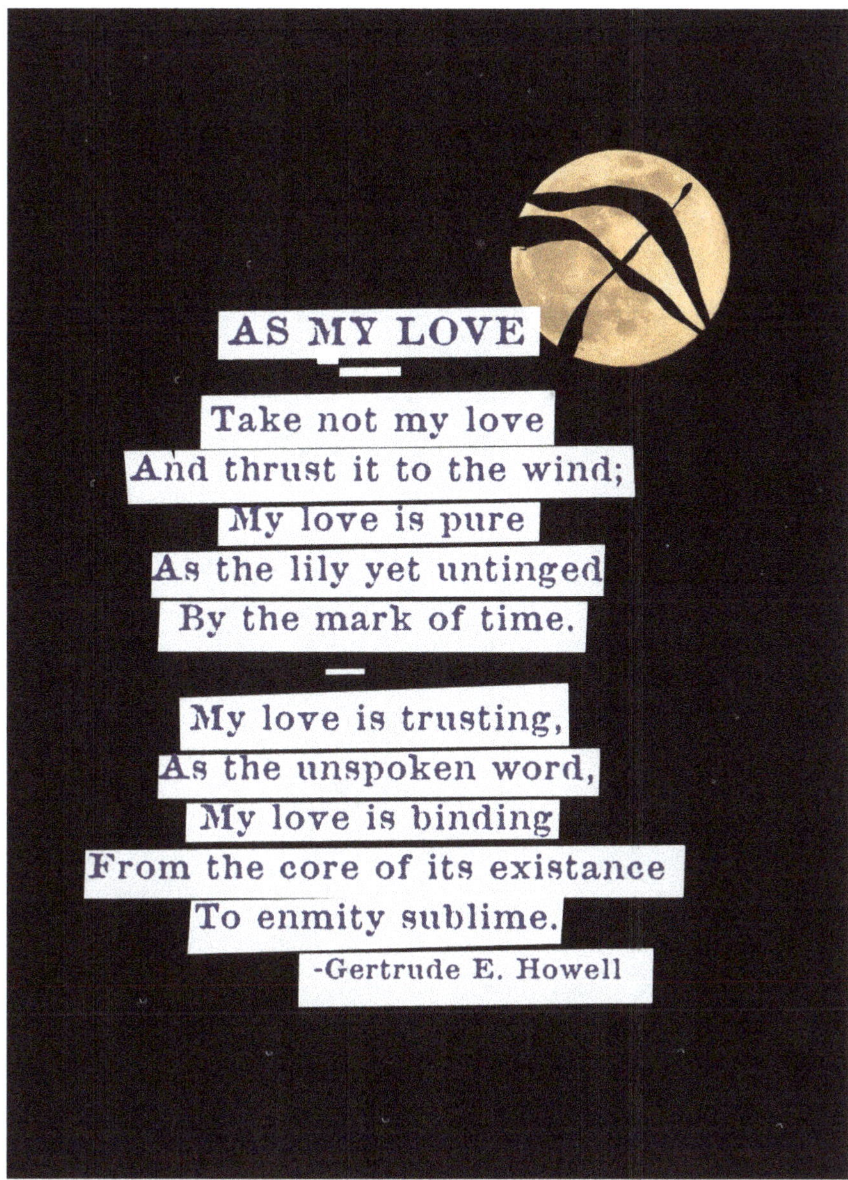

AS MY LOVE

Take not my love
And thrust it to the wind;
My love is pure
As the lily yet untinged
By the mark of time.

My love is trusting,
As the unspoken word,
My love is binding
From the core of its existance
To enmity sublime.

-Gertrude E. Howell

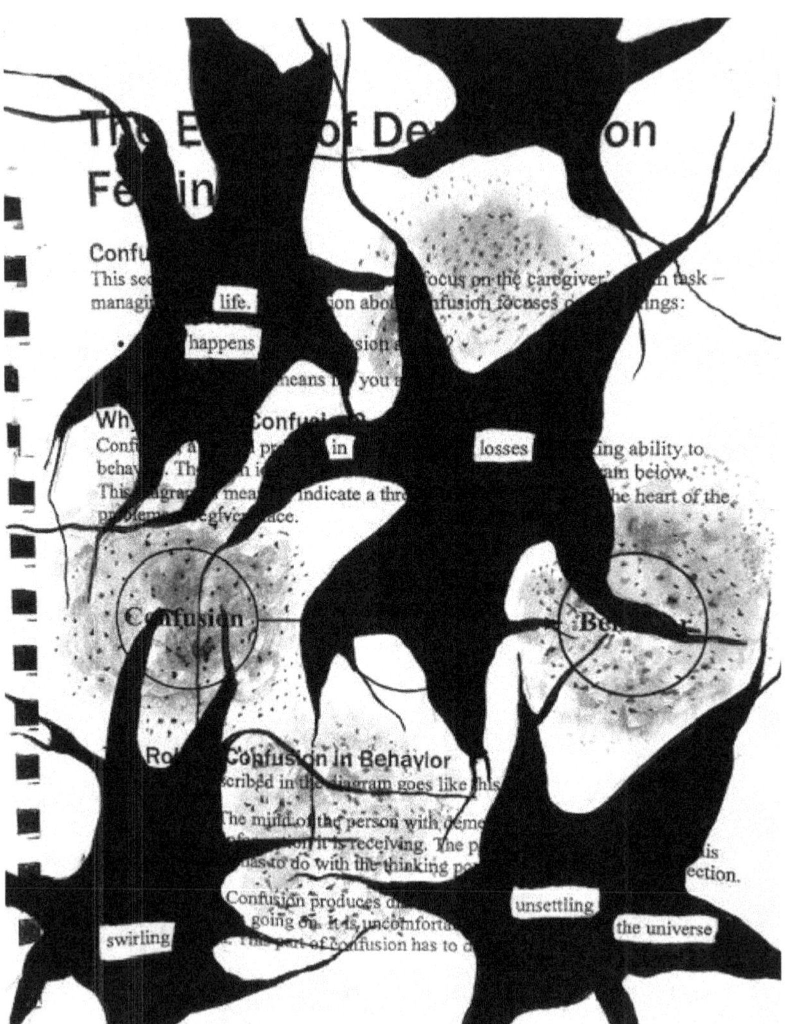
life.
happens
in
losses
Confusion
Behavior
Confusion in Behavior
swirling
unsettling
the universe

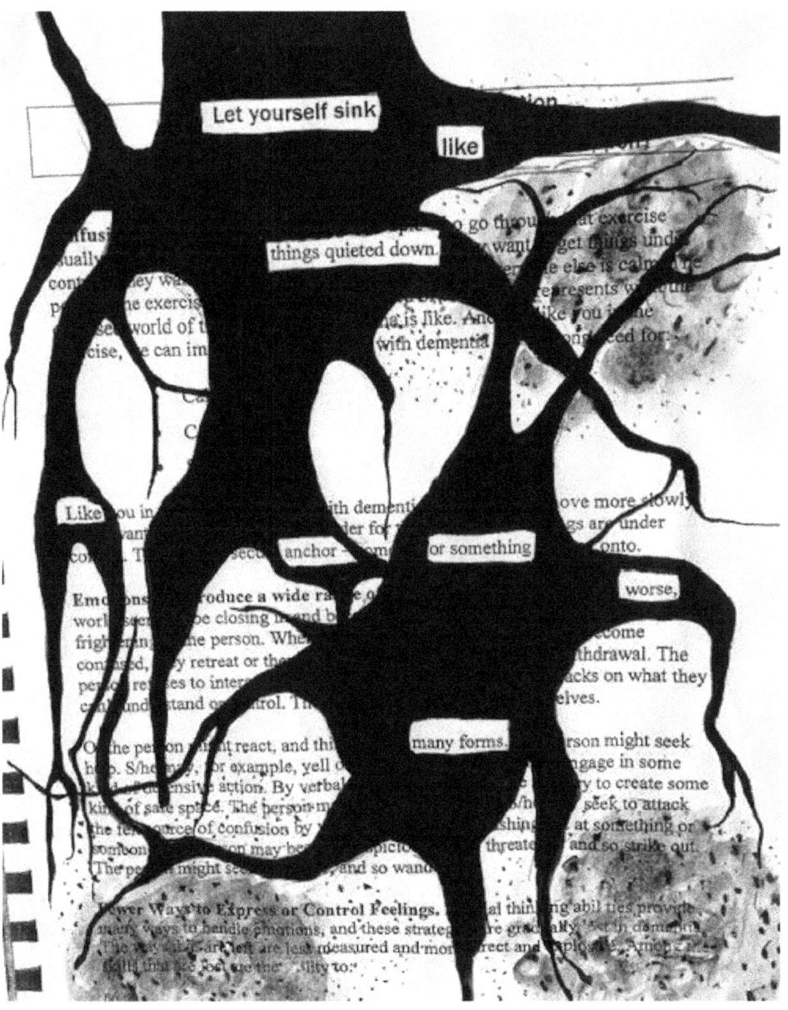
Let yourself sink
like
things quieted down.
with dementia
Like you in
anchor
or something
worse,
many forms.

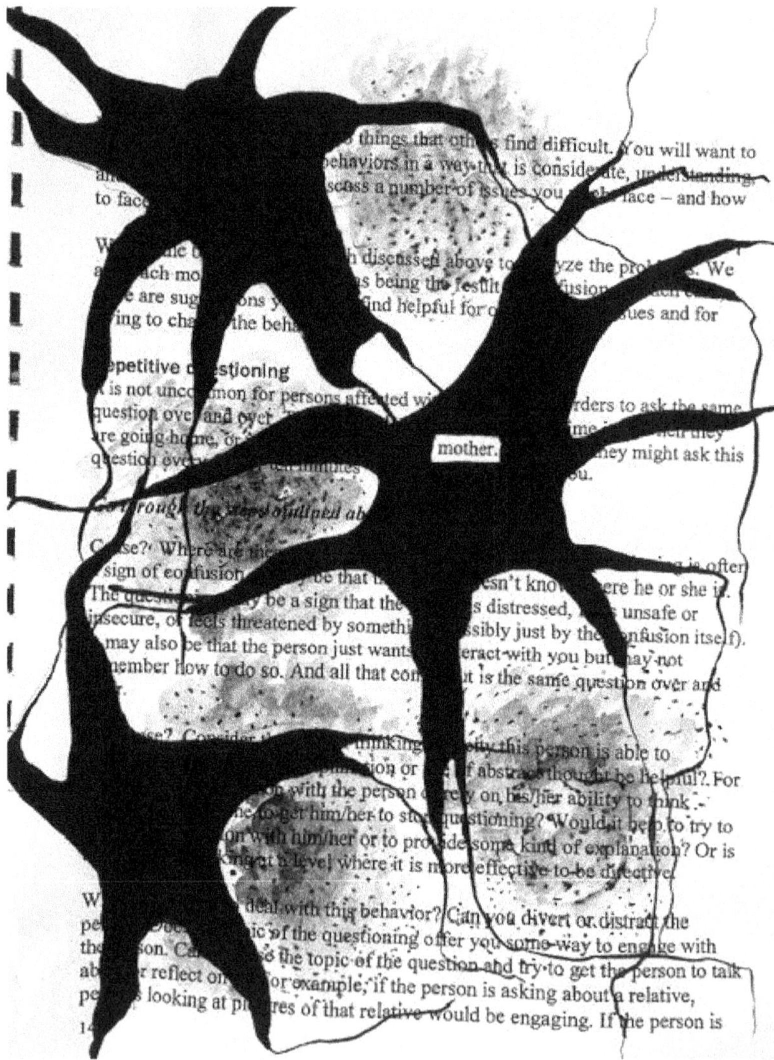

a role
a scene   will repeat
the scene
the role
alone.
A
Shadow
149

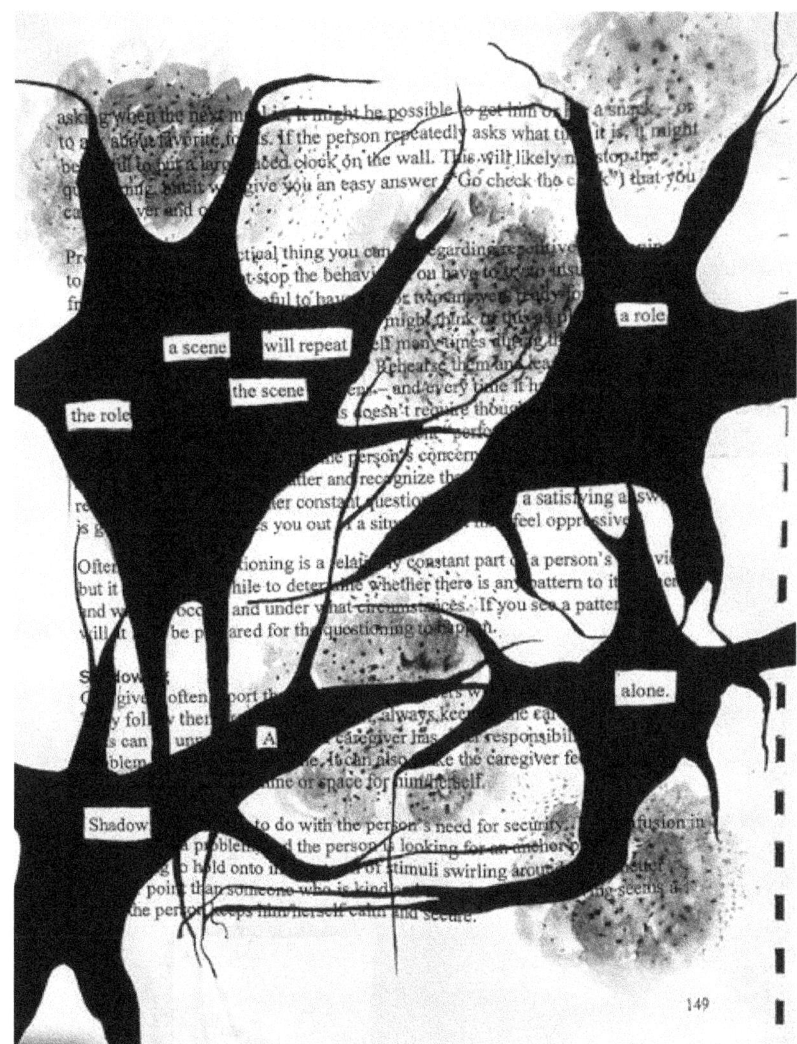

47

It's Always the Same Today

I saw you by the train again today. It was as if you never left. White sneakers. Black shirt. Blue jeans like a babe. You smiled like you do— which is barely. You smiled like it never happened.

I thought I remembered but now I'm not so sure. I haven't heard a word come out of your mouth in days. The last time was Tuesday on the phone with your mother—at least I think it was your mother. It could have been your girlfriend or your wife if you're into that kind of thing. You never told me. I didn't think to ask. I'm used to it. This. You. I like to think you remember me and part of me is certain that you do. But again, who's to know? I can't help it. I'm really very sensitive. Can't you tell? This is all to say— I think I love you. Is it that obvious? It's disgusting. Sometimes I stare at you so hard and also so discreetly that you almost don't exist. Maybe you're seeing me for the first time. In that case, here's my number. If I were someone who did that kind of thing. That is — give out my number. But I don't. I wish I did. This would be a lot easier if I did. It's easy for you. Easier. It's easy for me too but not as much. But also, who said I was easy? You. I remember your feet. Toenails too long even for me and my taste. I remember the dirt. You can't be all bad. Just some parts. Although, I am. I like your belt today. I haven't seen this one. It's usually brown with a silver round buckle—today's buckle is square. I can't tell if I love or hate your leather messenger bag. I find it simultaneously super lame and seductive. You look like you get the hardcopy of the newspaper. Like you annotate your feelings. Do you? Wait, don't answer that. I don't want to know. I like not knowing. You look like you eat hard boiled eggs in the morning and that you always scald yourself with your Colombian blend coffee. You can't help it. It's always just a little too hot. You drink it out of a mug that says "BOSS." You go to work and you like your job. You don't stir the pot. You think you're good. You think you know who you are and what you're all about. She thinks so, too. I'm sure of all this. Like I am of you. You try to love as hard as the movies showed you when you were twelve and thirteen, just birthing into your body. You never had acne as a kid. You were pretty blessed. You still are. If I could

measure your body again, I would. Your limbs telling mine to shut
the fuck up. If I could smell your dulled egg breath one more time, I
might. You look good. Did I say that already? It's always the same
but different watching you walk away. I have something to tell you,
though. Something I didn't get the chance to say. So, I'll see you here
tomorrow, right?

ANN HUDSON

Five

Every night you're gone
your brother shuffles in

and flops down on our bed,
stares at the cobwebbed ceiling.

How much longer will they
be there? or How did this

start? or How sick
are they? One question,

that's it, and then he rolls
over, complains about math,

or asks if we can order
pizza tomorrow night,

or begs for another
video game. On a scale

of one to ten, how
anxious are you? I ask

every few weeks.
Pandemic, remote

school, his grandfather
undergoing chemo,

a sibling in treatment…
I'm at about a twenty-one.

Five, he says. I'm at a five,
and kisses me on my cheek,

then pads into his bedroom
and closes the door,

the bar of light shining
adamantly against the floor.

MARK WALSH

Look Both Ways Before Crossing

The inner eye invites the dawn.

An over-dun landscape
crowns in its twiggy austerity -
against the hedgerow.

Even the sun's a double glance,
angling low and sharp
like an overcharged footlight,
polishing the hawk's spiked wings,
the squirrel's fur.

PAM MATZ

Hawk Held by a Woman

*After Bodleian Library, MS. Bodley 764, Folio 76v,
early 13th century*

We choose the moment
to beat our drums to startle
ducks into flight.

We have only the drums, the sack,
and the clothes we are wearing.

Mother has her own clothes,
the leather for binding her wrist,
the hawk, and her accord with the hawk,
which we do not share.

The hawk must be willing
to wrench the duck from the air
and give the duck to Mother.

So much can go wrong.
Sometimes the hawk nips her neck.

Sometimes we dream
the hawk's feathers are red and we are flying.

When Mother puts the first duck
into the sack
relief makes her tender.

MARIA SURRICCHIO

My Father, His Story

Campobasso, Italy, 1937

Spires of San Pietro slice
the noon sun in the alley
where two small boys

hide from the chores
of parents and priests.
Toes in the dust, knees

touching, they are just feet
away from where black shirts
will march in the square

a few years later. A few more
and they will wait on the corner
to sell their labor by the day

for too little
given how much it costs them.
So they pack bags

and a handful of earth,
and cross different seas
for other lives.

But that afternoon
in gold light flecked with salt
from the Adriatic,

each pulls a crust
from his pocket
and they press them together,

the olive oil
on one
anointing the other.

JOHN SIBLEY WILLIAMS

sky burial

*"I looked at photographs and suddenly understood that a photograph
was a letter to someone in the future."*
        —rick barot

during the pandemic, the bodies poured over
into mass graves. the graves poured over into

language. the language poured over into distrust
of everyone we once loved, even those who resemble us.

during the pandemic, my mother was still dead.
& when i held out two fists, my children discovered

a coin in neither. the plastic rosaries the old folks
fingered like money became money. the world

washed its hands. almost bloodless. the flesh gone all hard
& cracked. during the pandemic, our dog could finally

swallow the sky he'd long prayed to with his teeth.
& his teeth sharpened on the darkness within us.

when my son interrogated a dead bird with a stick
i read the gesture like scripture. i understood

there's only so much horror a body can take. only so much
song a mouth can hold before a few notes slip out.

during the pandemic, i thought of pompeii & how beautiful
a family frozen together in time. my father separated

from touch by double-paned glass. his parkinson's not the only
reason for tremble & tear. & my daughter asking the difference

between predator & scavenger. long before the pandemic,
we didn't believe in pandemics. or twilight. or palindromes.

how could absence read the same backwards? how could these
old wartime photos resemble our city today? & the vultures

carrying our scraps off to heaven, willingly, before the pandemic, we called
transmigration. son, father, wolf, i don't know what we'll sing from tomorrow.

SUSAN RICH

Praise the World to the Angel

I want a stanza with room enough
for the color of morning

glories iridescing into their own
cathedral of light—which welcomes

the waft of coffee and the alleyways
muraled with dangerous memories

I wish to relive. When evening
comes I plan to write an admiring letter

to the lipsticked woman outside
my gate in the threadbare coat, scarf

shimmering over her shoulders
attuned to whatnots and wonders.

Almond Joys for everyone!
In my notes, each sentence

arrives in light gold
dust assuring that each of us

must tend our better selves—
to say *thank you,* say *you're welcome,*

say *gesundheit.* I offer the congregation cinnamon
oatmeal with a whorl

of blueberries. This is the moment
when we become fruit citizens—

blueberry passports for everyone!
No teargas or bullets in my country,

just the sound of the refrigerator door
and the pine siskins chanting each to each,

the coil of cats wrapped in their own
prayers of star snacks and jasmine

because every poem needs jasmine
and a hope chest of scented wishes

that perhaps the angel might answer,
if we approach her bravely enough.

The Problem with Angels

Hollow bones weigh
less than a human heart.

They must choose between
wings or opposable thumbs,

good enough to love the world,
but too good to touch it.

The taste of feathers never
washes off their tongues.

No whiskey or lemonade
can banish it. They thirst for

something they can't name,
something that tastes of morning glories,

hibiscus. The bees wriggle into
silk, blue with agonies of white.

On Wednesdays their hands
break like the cardinal

lying on the roadside. On Sundays,
they give me the hedge clippers

and I raze their wing buds
back to the shoulders.

Blood and bone meal
under the roses—blooms

of paper yellow and a quiet,
private pink. They spend Mondays

on the front porch, tender,
thirsty. *Araneus marmoreous*

spins her two-foot web between
the fuchsias and the pansies.

PHOEBE REEVES

Limited Engagement, Las Vegas

Passion in the desert, jackdaw and dun hare
in crouch, with cower, cower coward.
Cows with spray paint on their flanks,
out flanked by upper air currents.

It's all live, folks, no time delay,
no dirty language now.
It's show time, it's 5…4…3…2…
Roll it, Benny. Get the shot—we
won't have a second chance.

The glass in the windows for 100 miles
will lie in splinters on the snow.

We're not in the desert anymore.
This is not a test. I repeat, this
is not a test.

PHOEBE REEVES

Before Uncle Schuyler's Cabin Burned

We would sit on the rough board steps up to the sleeping loft,
adults settled on the old overstuffed couch

and rattan chairs below us. Oil lamps in their fragile hurricane glass,
smell of patchouli, sweat, coffee grounds.

After a while they forget us and talk
of real things, through beer and cigarettes.

We walk the absolute country dark
back to our house, following the faint light

of our sneakers along the path,
slapping at mosquitoes.

You think these moments are nothing
when they come—

the quiet conversation, a candle
guttering in a pool of wax—

but even now you smell incense,
wood smoke in the dark of your sleepless nights.

Thoughts on the Large Hadron Collider

How tacky, the dogwood drooling blossoms everywhere,
while in his bower the bee regurgitates his honey.

Sea salt and iodine keep us all pretty goiter free
these days, but belligerent. Belligerent and taxed

at a higher rate for our necessary research & development.
Our necessary atom splitting and the labeling

of each particulate residue lingering in the smasher
nanoseconds, precipitating imaginary black holes

and a trillion mirror image honey combs
we reject, a trillion messy flowers we ignore.

PHOEBE REEVES

Amber Fingers

Pry into unopened
chrysalises, restless secrets
disturbing wet wings, elastic threads unfolding.

The rescinded damp of the desert.
The hot wet lips of the Queen Anne's Lace
folding her froth over alfalfa.

Mildew grasps the basement walls like an inappropriate
lover, heedless of the watching guests, fumbling
to unto cold cement.

In a burnt capital, cardinal directions
point only to ash. The wood thrush
weaves through a wilderness of char.

PHOEBE REEVES

This Shaking is Not Fear, It's Anger

What comes is in the smell of grass, wind
pushing blade on blade like a prow.

It approaches, oil over ocean
in a gale, with Category Five.

What comes now is as forewarning: Odysseus
treading water in the wine dark sea, an oracle

crumbling under acid rain, a harp played by waves
that push it ever farther up the shore.

House Wife

A woman's body rises up out of the ground. A woman's body rises up
out of the grass, up out of the gutter, out of the bathtub. A woman's
body rises up out of the grocery's magazine rack. Her breasts are
screen printed on recycled paper. Her breasts are blue and green.

A woman's body is not a loaf of bread. A woman's body is not the sun.
A woman's body is not the dirt. The woman's body is not a measure.
The woman's body is not a stone. The woman's body is not the moon,
is not the blood, is not her fingers in the dough.

The woman is a coat hook, a cat nap, a shockwave. She is a shelf of
jam jars, a fish pond, a farmhouse. She is a checkbook, a spreadsheet, a
stretchmark. The woman is her sleep, her toenails, her bile. The wom-
an leaves her sleep, her toenails, her bile. The woman leaves behind
her fingers in the dough. She leaves the moon, she leaves the blood, the
heart, the feet. She leaves the magazines in their luminescent displays.

She leaves the sun's pursuit, the sun's relentless burning. She rises out
of the sun, where she leaves her fingers pressed in the blood, her fingers
digging in the ground, her fingers buried in the gravel, the roots, the
chicken shit. The woman's body rises up out of the barn's broad splin-
ters. The field, her fingers on the radishes, her fingers pulling.

The woman rises up out of the past tense, leaves the event horizon,
leaves relativity, leaves Einstein and Archimedes doing math in the
bathtub. She is tired. Her fingers ache, her feet ache. She leaves
behind her ache. She leaves her branches, her chlorophyll, her solace.
She leaves her smokestack, her loading dock, her rotting pallets
on the asphalt.

She rises up out of her cities, her stairwells full of graffiti. She rises up
from where she fell when she tripped, when she waited with her nose
pressed to the dust while footsteps echoed. She waited while the sun
pierced her eardrums with honey, while the sun pieced together her
hair, while the sun swung centrifugal to her apex.

She leaves the sun hanging at an apex that can't come down. She has risen up and she can't come down. She leaves the moon in its own shadow, waiting for solstice. She leaves the moon touching its own footprints. She leaves the moon to trace its scars. She leaves the Stolichnaya, the Jack Daniels, the Bombay. She leaves lemons and cucumbers and pears. She leaves the hairbrush, the toothbrush, the stockings.

She rises up out of her skin, her muscle, her bone. She is silent, she is culpable. She rises up out of her desire, out of her hips, out of her fingers pulling the dough.

PHOEBE REEVES

Guide to Native Species of the Adirondacks

You touch a blade of grass at the pond's edge.
It could be rattlesnake manna grass. It could be
soft fox sedge, or the left margin of a dictionary page.
You forgot your glasses this time. You don't know
what to call anything, anymore. You don't know why
there are more named than there are living.

IN THE EYE OF

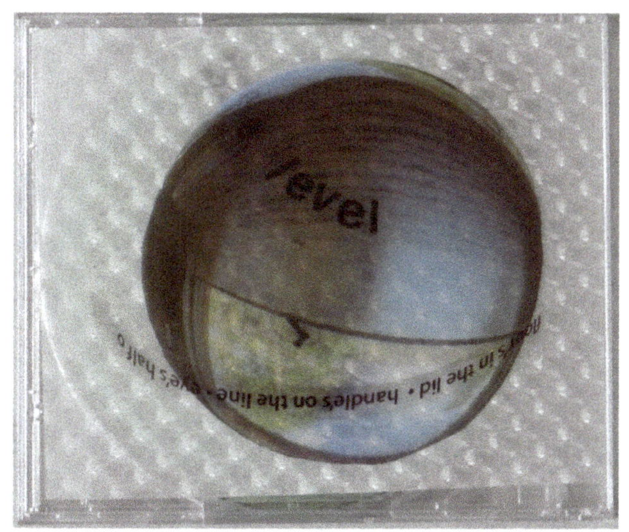

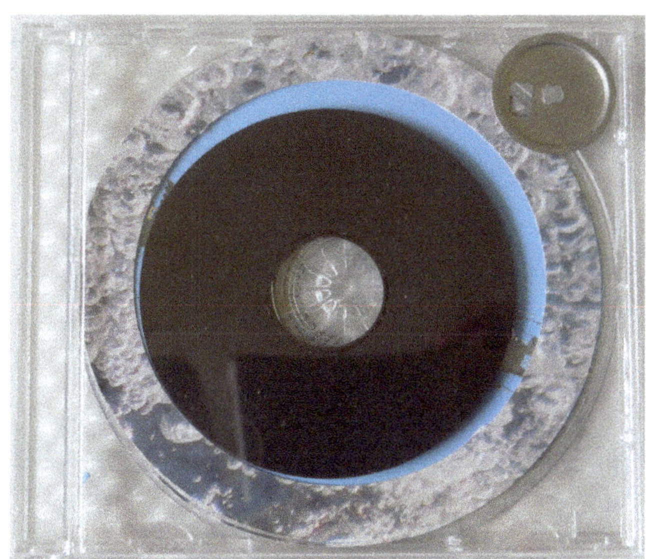

EYES EYING

ALONG THESE LINES MOVED

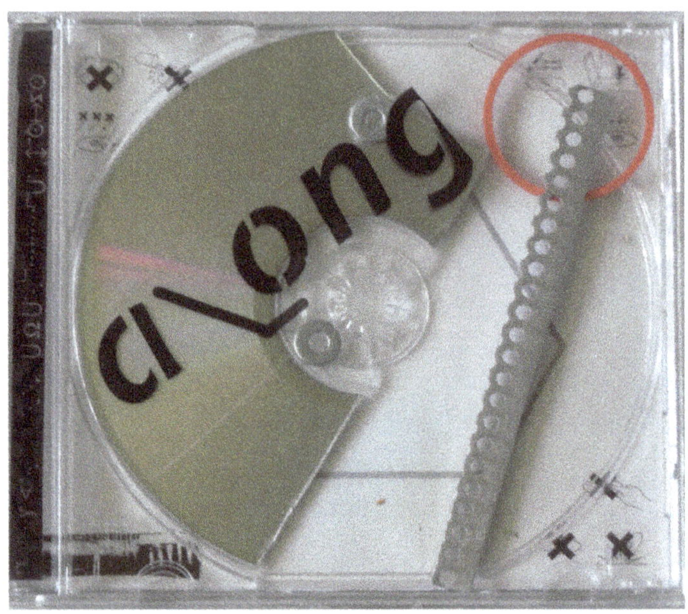

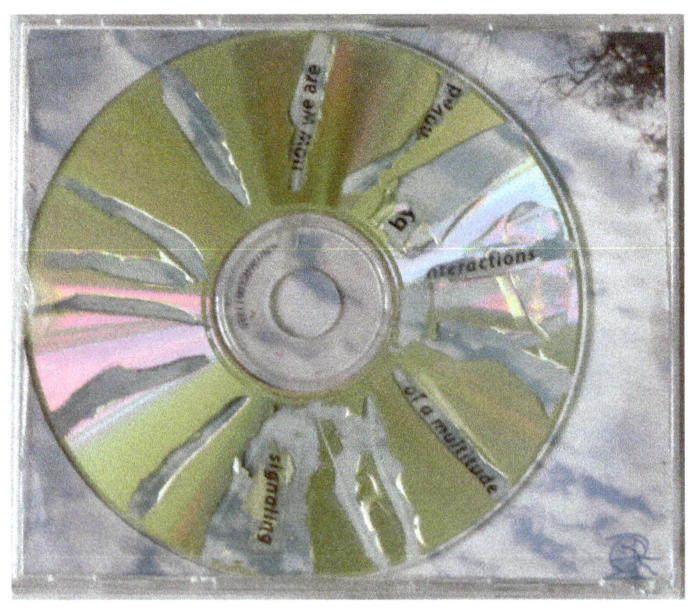

ROS ZIMMERMANN   from ..(ontinued distuR baN(eS·//r s /

IN A FOG ATLAS

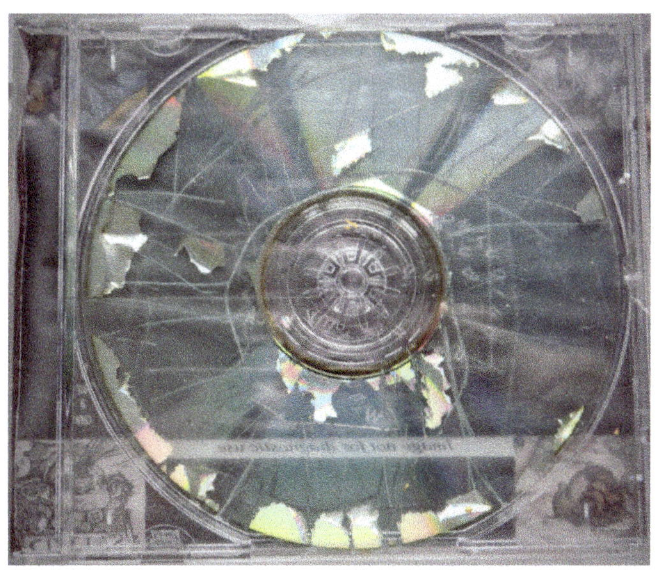

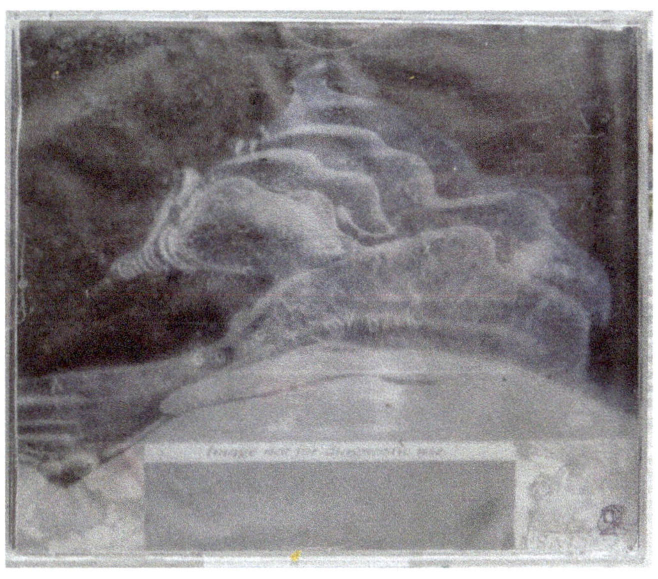

MIRIAM LEVINE

Dead Love

Where the last snow melted the soil is wet and black
as it was when we first met. Now you are back,
talking, talking, talking. Though you are dead,
you tell me you are surfing at Diamond Head,
riding the wet face of an enormous blue wave,
hard muscled, god-like, brave. I hear the wave
collapsed in the backwash, your voice, "Cashmere
for me was cut to order in Hong Kong. Dear
heart," your voice surges. "A woman taught me
all I know about fucking. I'll show you. See."
My has-been, how I once listened
endlessly to you. My lips glistened,
iridescent burnt sienna. We bit
and sucked. I lived in you. Eely tongue, it
kills me, your scent, a mix of salty musk and bourbon.
If we had forgiven would we have to go on and on?

JESSICA PURDY

Dear Morpheus,

This morning I didn't take the time
to linger in your message. Would you
please send it again? I want to feel
the edges of your dream-bricks,
the way morals take no part
in what happens there. I've found
love where there was none, lost
people to future events. When I'm
drowsy please let me read your letters.
I've had to watch as the TV forms
nuanced portraits of concern and doubt.
Contained ships of grief. Bubbles
of pink spew and grassy hills that tirade
their muddy haunches across my hips.
I want to get out and sever the neck
off a champagne bottle. Spray the hull
of the ship with my celebration. Want
to gasp and fever match a chess game.
A chest game? Perhaps with longing
you can come to me, confess everything.
I will listen to what you know. Give me
original tangerines and marvelous
puppets with invisible strings. Kites
to clouds and rivers that rise up
with hand-drawn dramas. I'd love
to know what you know. Why you
take your time to show me the dead
as if they're right in front of me. Versions
of life and those tactile sounds they make.
Show me why I can't have the loves I have.

ANASTASIA VASSOS

je t'aime

we occur as glued friends
Jacques Cousteau & I
deep blue explorers
industrious water striders
the Aegean calls us
waves conflate *tong* & *tongue*
our arms stroke salt
in time to inhalation/exhalation
our fluent *lingua franca*

ABBIE DOLL

Flesh Concoctions

Agnes is a seamstress. She sews the skin of every unborn child, mapping out their future with freckles, moles, and wrinkles, stitching trillions of cells one by one until arriving at an end result as unique as the individual. Palms are her favorite; each one begins as an empty fleshy canvas, a rectangular chunk ready to accept her big sweeping brushstrokes; she floods the open space with an endless maze of tiny intersecting streams and tributaries. The joint markings beneath our knuckles may make each finger appear to be attached by a mere stitch or two, but Agnes spends days upon days developing her designs to the brink of painstaking perfection.

Agnes creates it all. She can tell you how well each of her creations will (or won't) moisturize and can even recite their future injuries on a cellular level. Drawing the significance behind every line is her domain. By sculpting skin, she weaves her stories, selecting spots for every scrape and bruise of childhood. Agnes' arthritic hands have been at this for thousands of years but have never once repeated themselves. She is proud of her work as a sorceress of skin, designing lives. Our body's largest organ is her world. Agnes maps out a lifetime of blackheads and ingrown hairs; she knows, all too well, where the body's blemishes hide.

First and foremost, skin protects; it's the official separator between our interior and every external threat. It is, at heart, the body's storyteller. It secretes stories, oozes oil and sweat. Agnes sutures the cells with incredible finesse, transforming them into an intricate honeycomb structure like a bed of doughy oyster crackers baking in the oven. She knows and feels it all—the pang from next week's sunburn, that sharp jolt when the knife slips, the dull throb from that blister on your heel, everything. She knows when a cancerous mole first surfaces and the second a cut becomes infected. Next time you pass a mirror or pause to study the secret specificity of your exterior, be sure to stop and express your thanks to the saint of skin.

LAUREN SAXON

Re: Ghosting

I am writing to you from inside a body that used to belong to you.
Which is to say, I am writing to you as love. Up and down, inch by inch.
Though I could be, I am not angry with you. Instead—

I am daydreaming. That you walk boldly into the restaurant where I work.
You are looking up to me, for once. Meeting my gaze. You say you
missed me, and you mean it *I can tell* that you mean it. Still. Rather than
melting into your arms or neck or lips, I don't respond. I keep a straight
face. I say *oh, did you* in a voice flat enough to keep my hurt both seen
and level.

Of course you will ask, then, if I am mad and I'll say *no* before you finish
the question. Tell you to have a seat at my bar. Pour you an ice water
without asking and *picture this*. Picture me, sliding the water slowly across
the countertop and *picture you*, smiling. Smiling because of me.

Now you will say sorry, and you will mean that too. With all your guilt,
seeping into the air around us. Despite having already forgiven you, I
might be cold again. I might say *it's fine* and you will say, quickly, that it
is not. I don't argue and this. This is the best part—

I will move, close enough to touch you. Close enough to brush your
hand, waist or cheek with my own I will say, *it's fine,* in a way that
suggests I am not done talking. You will be so close to me and I will tell
you this.

Tell you what I've rehearsed in this daydream and the one before and
the one before that, I will say— *I love you. So much more than you love me.*
And sometimes it shows. And sometimes it hurts.

You will be quiet because we both know this is true. Again, there is
nothing to argue.

Here is where the dream diverges. Where I spend most of my day,
deciding what to do next. What to do after you hear *I love you more.*
There are two choices.

The first, the one that I choose nine times out of ten, is to admit that I am trying. Admit that I am working hard to give only what I receive. Admit it's hard sometimes—getting so little from you.

My eyes will be downcast as I say this. I will laugh it off. I will lie. Maybe say— *don't worry, I am a little less in love each day.* I could give you a drink stronger than water. I could forget your straw and hope that you forget this conversation, we will go home. And fall asleep in separate beds, while this sounds safe.

There is another option. A second one. It cannot happen without your consent. Which is to say— I will ask, nicely, before kissing you. I will wait for you to pull away and hope that you do not.

Again, I could give you a drink stronger than water. I could remember your straw and you would remember that I love you, *we will go home.* And I will hold you, as close as you will let me.

My ending— is entirely up to you. I am so much yours, that even my dreams are yours to dictate.

Take your time.

TINA SCHUMANN

Body and Soul

> *"You don't have a soul, Doctor. You are a soul. You have a*
> *body, temporarily."*
>
> —A Canticle for Leibowitz.

Such perverse parasites are we,
collapsing into each other

night after night,
disruptive and heretical.

Though compliant
as Russian dolls.

Corporeal keeper
of our carnage.

Clatter kitchen
and comfort couch.

Soft box, satchel
and scullery maid.

Primped and propped.
Test subject

and meat puppet.
Judas and Jezebel

incarnate. Body obscura,
body of knowledge.

My cathedral,
my cloister, rectory

and nave, fun house
and asylum.

Straight talker
and midnight.

TINA SCHUMANN

That Feeling You're Feeling is Called Languishing.

Not as in linger or languid, evoking

    a long-legged sunbather half asleep

on her lounge chair. Lacquered nails

dangling off a limpid hand, long

    and lax as a diving board

poised this close to a Margarita sweating in the sun.

    No, I am thinking more of a slow

        stupor. Stoned to the bone –

non-responsive floating; the towels lift

and drift into humid air, softly bumping

    the topiaries. All sound is buffeted

by cotton batting and diminished

    like a transistor radio thrown

off the banks of a minor river

    in another state.

Bowie is practically yelling

    but you cannot decipher the song.

Some small part of you still believes

    you will return

to a time when you were feeling

    all the feels. The hotel pool wavering

in technicolor blue, the song coming

    at you in stereo. In stereo.

FIONA WILKES

Music Box

I did not ask to be a dancer.

I cried when they nailed my slippers to the floor and pinned my arms above my head. Every four seconds the mirror taunted me, my mouth rounded like a rose, ready to sing my melody.

I was a gift for an ungrateful niece, who opened me only when her fawning friends visited. "My aunt sent me this from Paris." She crowed and they would respond as if I were a fireworks show. She twisted my golden key much too tight and with a jolt, I would turn for them. My song was always repetitive, although even I must admit it is pretty.

She handed me down to her daughter, who put me in a drawer and forgot I was there. I was grateful for the reprieve, although I was haunted by my song, even in the darkness, even as I lay folded down, cramping, always ready to spring up into an elegant pirouette.

When the daughter died, her granddaughter uncovered me. She was gentle when she pried open my ancient roof, oiling my key before she dared turn it. She showed me to her husband, "Look at her. She must be a hundred years old."

I'd like to tell her I am older than that, but a lady never reveals her age; especially when her mouth is painted on and her voice is carved into an ancient record.

"Does it still work?" Her husband asked, peering at my chipped paint. "Turn the key."

She did as he asked and, with just a moment's hesitation, I started to twirl. My peeling paint looked so sad in the tarnished mirror, but when I began to sing, I was as young as the day I was made.

ACE BOGGESS

Heidegger Conference

Went to the event as if it was a Broadway musical.
I had finished school & didn't need this,
though I *needed* it, or anything
with no fee for admission.
Life's costly. I had shortfalls.
I should've fought for wisdom,
instead fixing on oily, sweet scents
of flavored coffee & doughnuts
carted out for guests at intermission.
Did my best, listening while academics
talked about versions of freedom,
what it means to go on living &
at what expense, at what expense.

SUSANA H. CASE

A History of Commitment

I was squirrelly in my twenties,
by which I mean unpredictable.
I wore peacock feather earrings,

mother-earth skirts, tried to save
money for harder times,
though usually I was broke. People

around me snorted coke.
Love veered away before impact,
a twitch away from being a traffic

accident. What happened in my thirties—
I hammered together lopsided
bookshelves, stuck them

in the mostly unused kitchen,
declared my cockroach farm *home*,
beat with a broom the man who tried

to crawl through the window,
until he gave up. Then I got metal bars
installed. The front door was metal too—

this was New York. I unlocked it for you
when the man who slept in the hallway
started shooting the ceiling lights.

DENISE BERGMAN

TV Blizzard

What lure, detached pixels
floating, unpredicted
Midday midtown Manhattan
a burst underground
steampipe geyser,
an asbestos blizzard
blanketing surface & crevice,
thick as talc on a baby's raw bottom
Breaking News all day
recaps, tumults, placations—
wrong-place-wrong-time pedestrians
fill yellow dumpsters
with clothes in sealed plastic bags,
maps of "hot zones" & cordoned-off streets,
experts claiming "safe trace levels"—
deadpan voices
hour by hour until late night
slides past Yankees extra innings,
winding down like the old Philco,
sitcom to news to Star Spangled Banner
to "Indian-head" test-pattern target
to lisping static lullaby
to blank screen.

EVELYN ENFIELD

Gladys Kravitz Assumes the Existence
of the Astral Body

The stars don't mean anything
yet. Her astral escape
is a moth circling—
star-dusted wings battling
the void, it's hard to know
how dark the moon's craters can get;
that it's a window she's really wanting—
sun-yellowed curtains in moonlight.

When will she
wisp her way through?
Think herself beyond next door's
red brick; listen to the after-dinner
rasp; hum along with those
peculiar bodies, wriggling noses,
spontaneously othering husbands—

Oh, Abner. The linoleum
smells of ether. The kitchen sink is
spilling over with small town
Dawn bubbles— She is far away
from the inky dark spilling from
her own backyard.

STEPHEN VINCENT

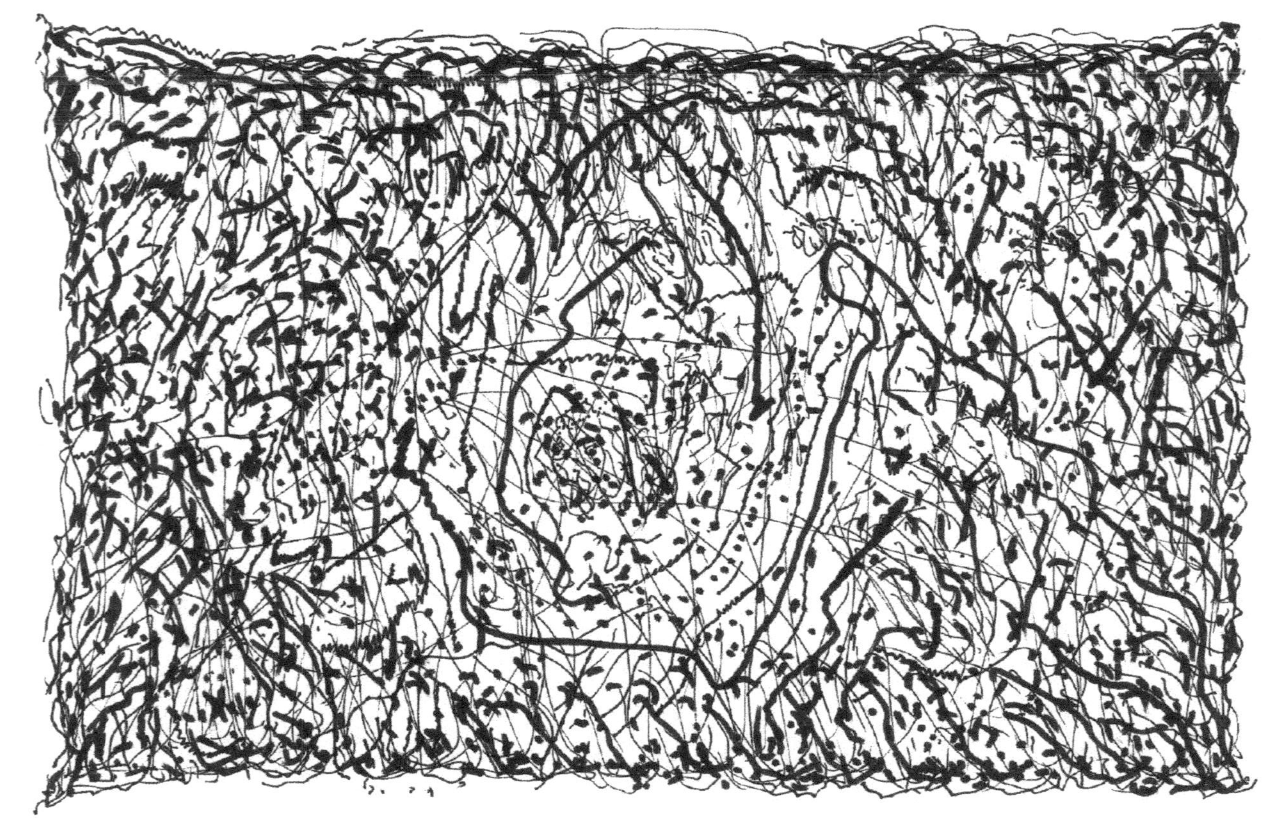

In these origins, the words radiate, ripple in the mud, the whirlpool within the maw. Occasionally, right to the point, the mud percolates to circle and shift its forward motion in and out from the pool's inner-edges. Within the poem words research each layer of grammar. Bachelor sentences are stripped bare, shaken at the heels, held to account by the toes. Arches rarely cave or crack. Full throated the poet circles from the shoulders to occasionally toss in the grace notes of a madrigal. An audience may want to believe they are in Church; rhythms spangle, a mouth opens larger and larger. Mercy. Mercy. The angels– words flutter – the whole poem opens to deliver.

Haptic #3/3: Beverly Dahlen Reading at her "Tribute" Celebration at Small Press Traffic, San Francisco; 12.13.2008

STEPHEN VINCENT

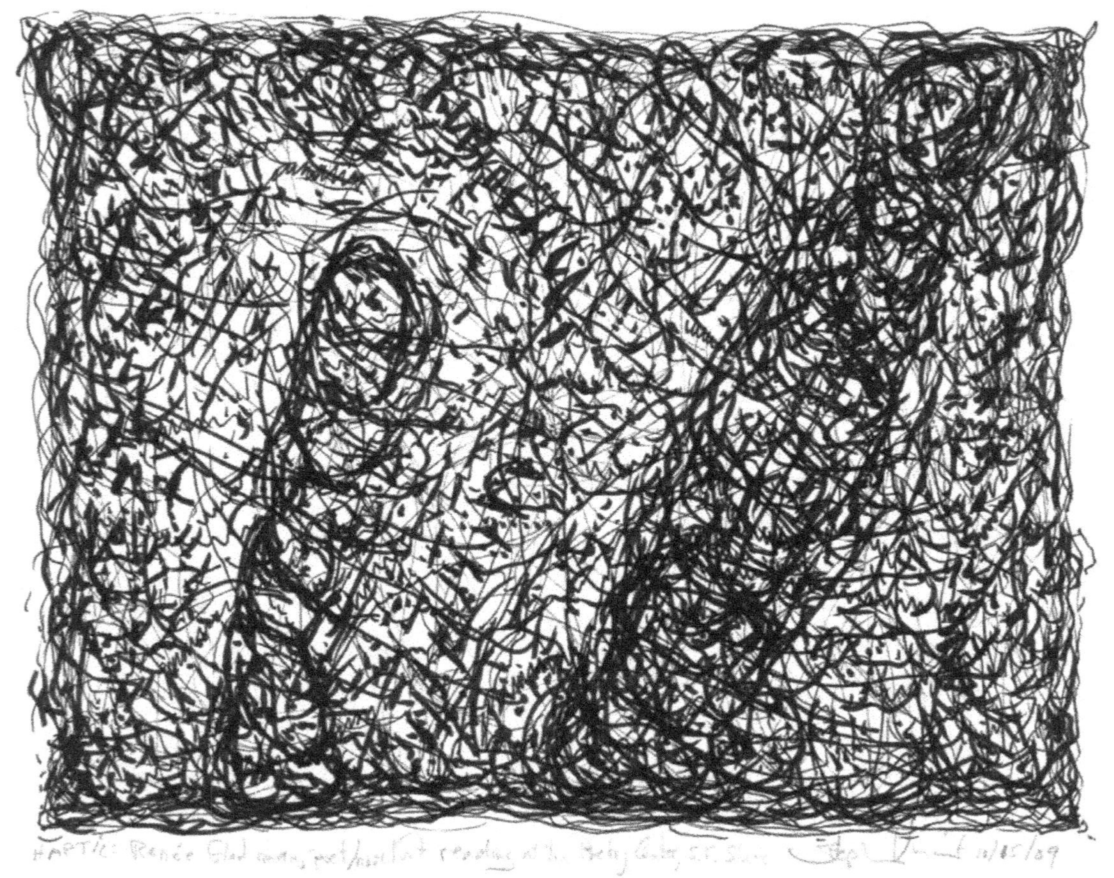

The dance of ghosts, where, shoulder to shoulder, trembling apparitions in white; we scout to play and write among them; intense language is our target; the demons, though some are kind, are relentless. We know not who they are. The sway of language is to keep a balance, to rise & weave parabolic threads into arcs to betray the thick underbrush. Who can say what we own? Who can say what they want? The winds will carve out terror, isolate meaning & perpetually trouble the lone walker. Words will scissor stitch a script into the night of the forest. Partnered with and against nocturnal forces for reasons the heart cannot know; we will never give up, nor submit. The poem feeds a childless wanderer.

Haptic: Renee Gladman, poet/novelist reading at the Poetry Center, San Francisco State 10.05.09

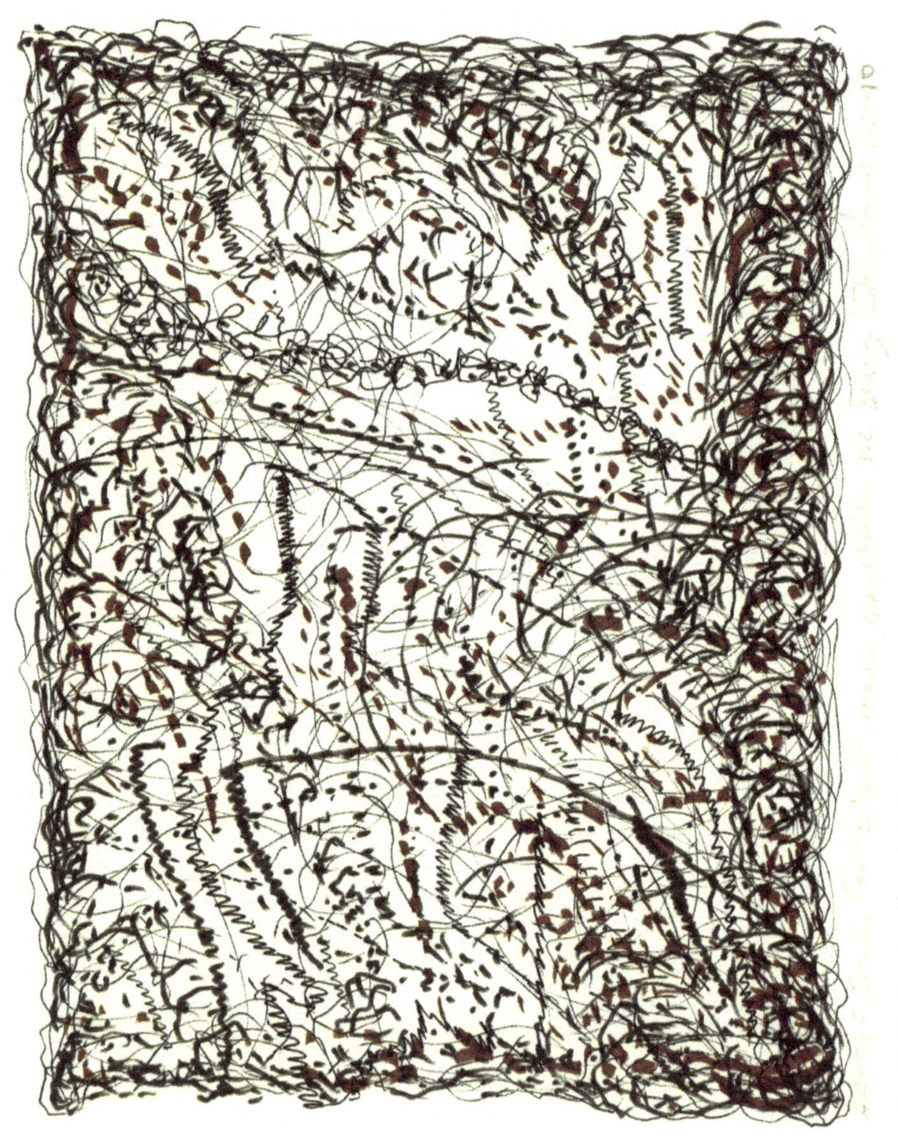

It is not really about the wind, the way say wind, when properly knotted into a spare series of parallel strings, will thread down and across a formerly blank space. No. Yes it remains simple in the way the winds do stretch and splay the strings in and out through the geometric shapes atop and within which a distinct rhythm invades while the ink moves variously to become story, to become relish. To make a story, a fabric where an un-tenuous wind breaks to pour behind and through.

Haptic: Brenda Coultas, poet, reading, Maude Fife Room, U.C. Berkeley 1.28.2010

Lion's Jaws

لله درُّ اللّيالي ما أحيسنها
وما أحيسن منها ليلةَ الأَحَدِ
لو كبتَ حاضرنا فيها وقَدْ غفلتْ
عينُ الرقيب فلمْ تنظرْ إى أحدِ
أبصرتَ شمسَ الضُّحَى في ساعدي قمرٍ
بل ريَم خازمةٍ في ساعَذْيْ أسدِ

God, turn on the nights,

    and which can best Sundays?

You should've seen us after the neglect

    of that drowsy, ancient chaperone:

Those nights I feel the morning sun pulsing my arms

    as I was a moonlit gazelle in the jaws of my lion.

—Translation by Will Pewitt

Sanctuary

أَلاَ لَيْتَ شِعْرِي هَلْ سَبِيلٌ لِخَلْوَةٍ

يُنَزَّهُ عَنْها سَمْعُ كُلّ مُرَاقِبِ

ويا عَجَباً أَشْتَاقُ خَلْوَةَ مَنْ غَدَا

ومَثْوَاهُ ما بَيْنَ الحَشَا والتَّرائِبِ

I'd hand over my poetry

    if it could buy us solitude,

        a getaway from all of the eyes

    that've seen more than they should.

If only Time gave us sanctuary,

    a recess in the tide of tomorrows,

        where you could finger the grass,

    and come to rest in this earth.

—Translation by Will Pewitt

CRAIG DOBSON

Helen, home

Taken and retaken:-
ten horned years goring their *petite mort*,

hating her as Troy had,
as the widows here do, their slight men

stealing her in dreams,
each dawn restoring her to reflection's

infallible rule –
the sly, elusive, blank-eyed paramour

making up
for the spoils of the night before.

COLIN JEFFREY MORRIS

Rescue (a whole that is not you)

Audubon's *Trumpeter Swan*

An undergoing, a slow-floating
creamy primitive

shaded the same shade
as deeper waters. An infidel

arrangement of curves
arrested by attention.

*

Observatory nerves increase
the thickness of the belly.

An open web diffuses
down the grassy element.

The motion pushes front
and in (as if) forced

by watery palms.

*

Adept of experience, native
on any ground – a plunge into

reality and through.

—for Stephen Piersant

COLIN JEFFREY MORRIS

Napoleon Crossing the Alps
Audubon's *Golden Eagle*

Allow the caged engine
its glare. Accept black-
throated bite. Assent
to tiger-snap. Let
slaughterhouse design,
admit the New World
leapers and jumpers. Catch
cutthroat arrangement
of claws. Confess natural-
born Bonaparte. Run
razor-thin steel the way
through him. Define prey,
eye-gouged, complicit.
Collect force, draw it sky-
ward across the numb
face. Present flight
to the rocks of its haunts.

MICHELLE BOLAND

Ecosystem

Clemency is a root
accepting decay,

how the soil shifts
now that the tree people
have cleaved and pulped
the camphor dying

at the edge of my father's lawn
from heart rot.
It doesn't matter

that mushroom conks
embittered the meat.

Or that my brother and I
stopped speaking
about the spores
seeping from its trunk

and relied on an arborist who
seemed too young
to weigh testimony
against another season.

No, what matters is that
I hardly cried the night long ago

when our mother
sped down the driveway,
killing our deaf cat.

Which is why
it was left to me

to surrender the tree
to the men's behemoth machine.
Because clemency
is finding a trick of the mind

to sluff off the weight
of our loss – the generations
of ants that will not know

its crannies for their winter nests,
the woodpecker
needing somewhere else
to steady herself as she drums.

It comes by remembering
the way I once wrapped
my arms around the camphor

and stood on its exposed roots
like a child dancing
on her father's feet,

glad for the means
to bolster my weight.

JULES JACOB

The Limnologist's Song

My granddaughter maps bacteria
in fatigued streams, sings *my constant*

friend to tide pools and freshwater bayous,
I know, I know when her booted feet

plunder mud-choked springs.
She serenades Lake Winnipesaukee,

why should I feel discouraged?
when she spots black rain,

because I'm happy swimming
to a plastic, magnetic letter Q

and *why should my heart be lonely*
as she weds it to her ring finger.

Before diving through algae blooms,
Oh, oh-oh because I'm free.

* *His Eye Is on the Sparrow* lyrics
  (italicized) by Civilla Durfee Martin

RENOIR GAITHER

The Tips of Rainbows

"Sun's out, pretty day,"
Sister would say—

wagoned along petitioning sidewalks,
chrysanthemums abloom on her eyelashes

mail carriers named every black dog Pal
and bluegrass, wherever it grew on the Southside

of Chicago, smelled like a river in the Congo
or dried sinsemilla

Pinky, alas, by the doorstep kept watch,
books of policy numbers in her jacket

Miss Ellis sighed, entombed in walls made stale
by the hot comb's grease and corner store chitlins

Someone hung the paper boy in the tree
across the street, and the block club took donations

Johnny Walker Red sat in the corner next to the pickled
olives as my mother played bridge with the Popes

on New Year's Eve, and smoke from our alley barrel
fire seemed to lure young men who wore floppy fedoras,

spat interminably, and showered everywhere
they drew breath with a quickening coolness

Every rainfall left us to wonder
where the rainbow fell, hidden behind

brownstone bracelets and monkey bars of street signs
that cued dreams of people we would never know

Sister said, "Sun's out, pretty day, Daddy,"
as the sidewalk held us up as high as we wished to go.

JENNIFER MARKELL

Some Things I Stole as a Child

Garnet, cinnamon sticks, map of lion habitat.
My mother's Evening in Paris
& a stranger's name, spelled backwards.
I was a thief of 3 blind mice & a dozen
curse words stashed in a jam jar
with pennies from heaven, a song
my father crooned when it rained.
Displaced, the lion roared,
its mane *unkempt,* my father said
of the latch-key girl in the apartment next door.
For her I stole a butterfly barrette.

Inside the lion something trembled,
afraid of itself, like a clock or a bomb.
I set the table with goblets & raw meat.
Where was home & what on earth
& who were these people
who called themselves a family?

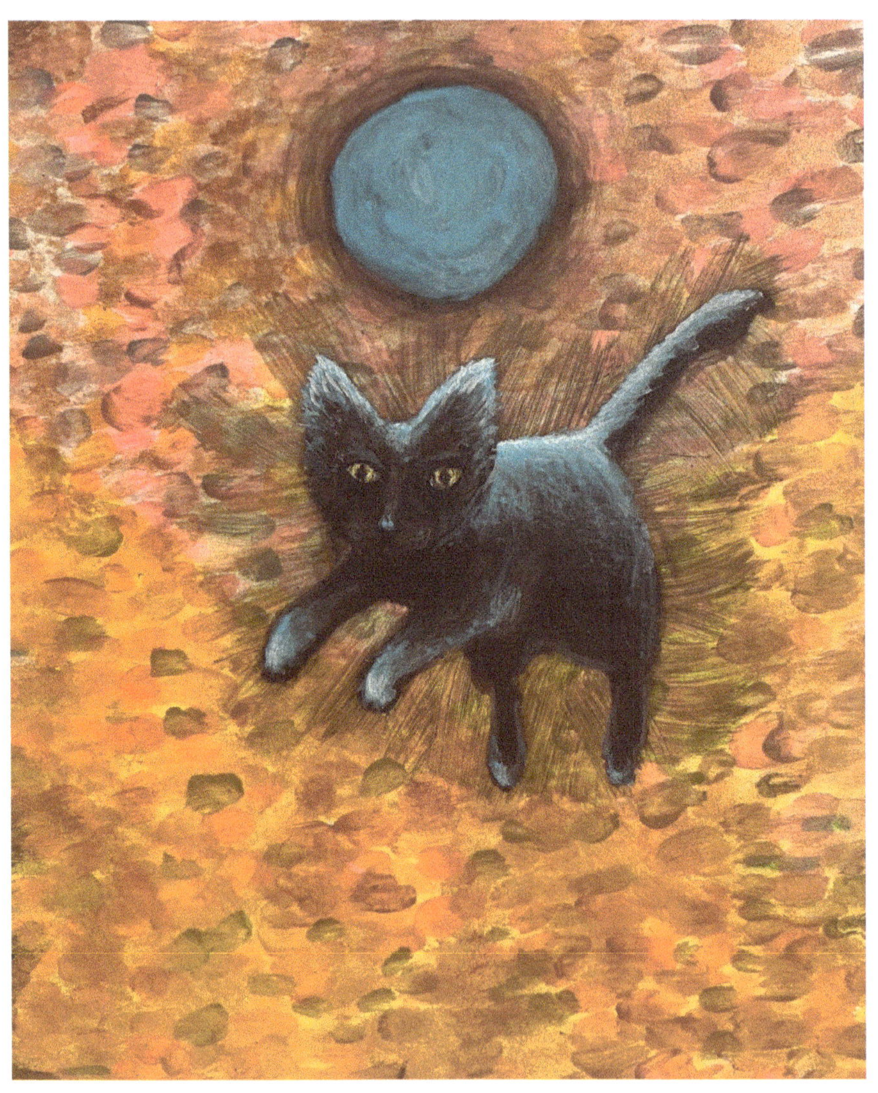

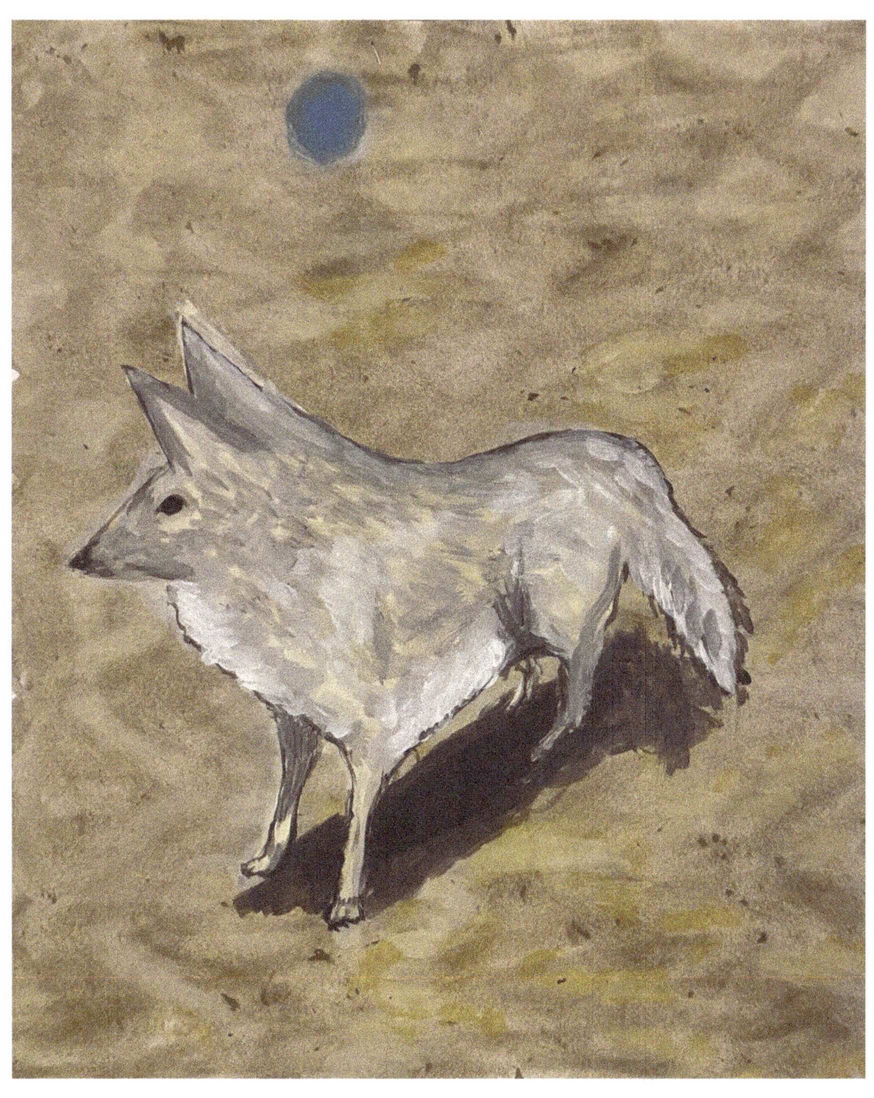

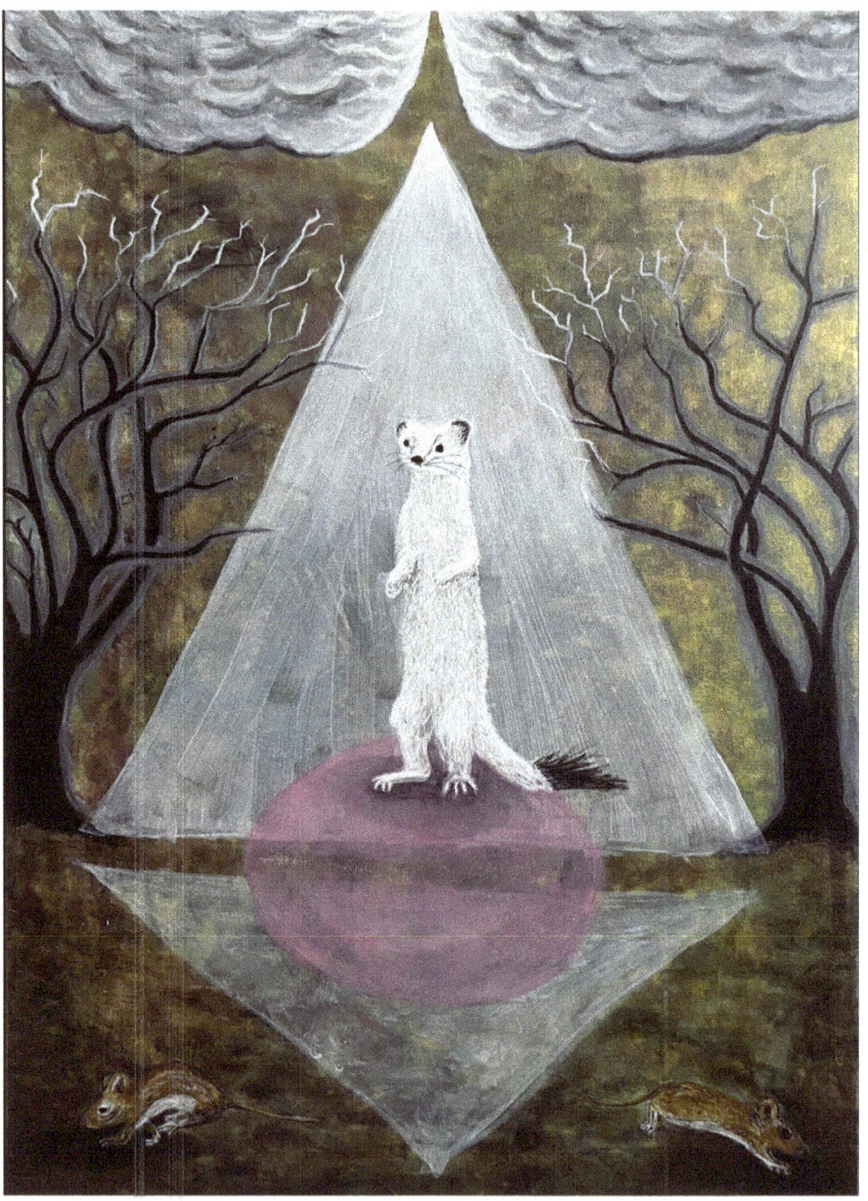

GILMORE TAMNY

Rabbit Dancing in Front of Fire with Books

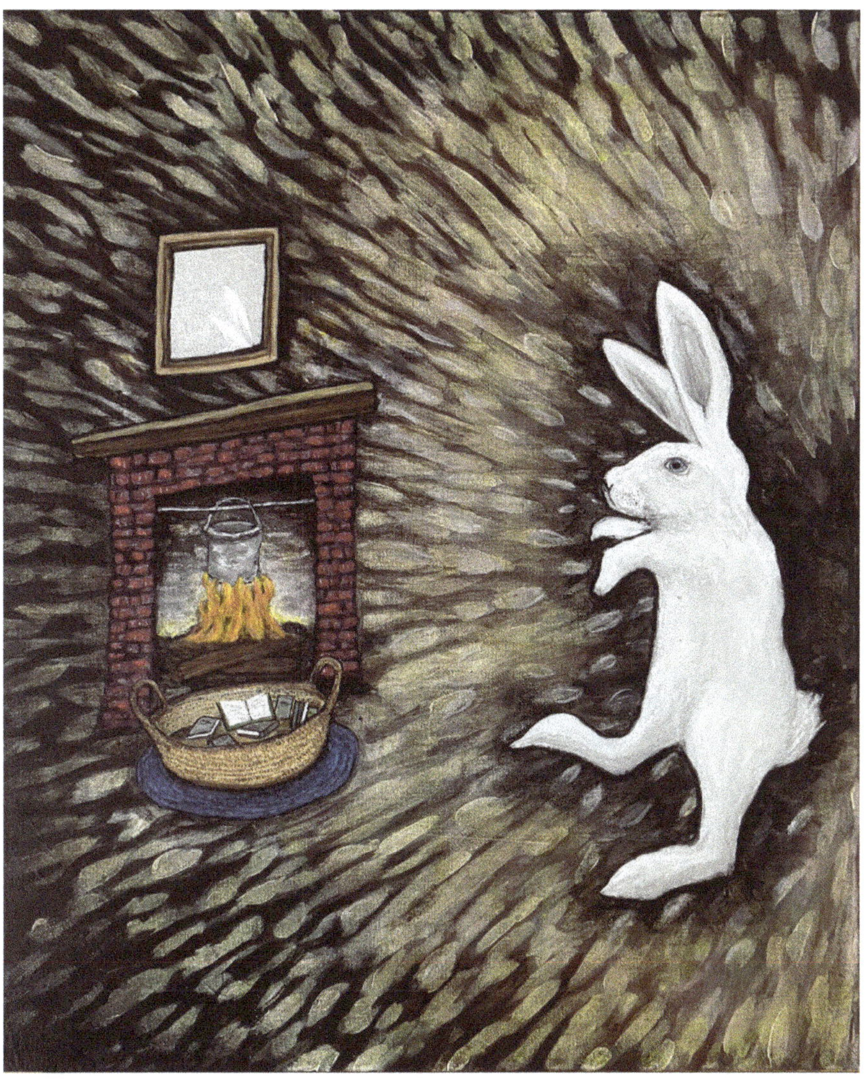

Squirrel with Acorn Stars

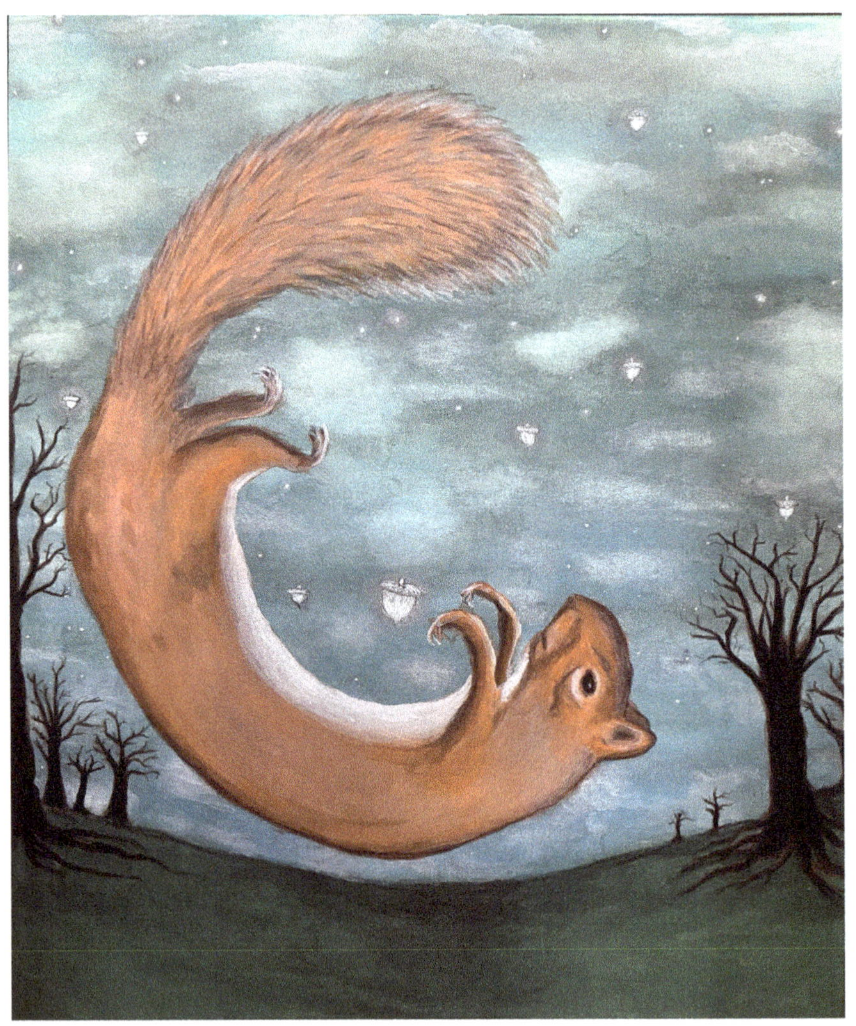

CRYSTAL C. KARLBERG

Ortolan

Cover my head with a napkin, I'm ready
to dine. At the altar of the black crown

my throat strikes white. The sight of many bats
covering the sky with wings

mutes me. What is honey to the bee-
eater other than sweet? In this citadel

of endless pines, call the night heron to
the swamp's edge; I have a spell to cast.

In the dark certain birds gorge on millet then
welcome the novocaine armagnac, tired of

the sound of their own chewing. Digest this
hammer if you can. All the yellow has been

flushed from the leaves. Branches create
connections (read: claves). Lanky, striolated, ghost-

pale. Turns out we are a territorial flock of blue
rolling in like waves. Red-backed, tree-creeping,

shrikes collect along the tower walls, their silhouettes
a silent caution. Lynx is the sheriff in these parts.

He is bright as moon and unafraid of wolves,
knows a delicacy when he sees one.

R. NEMO HILL

Late Apples

Some die young.
Some barely blush
then dip and drop
to rot in the rush
of wind through wet grass.

Brief stains
on green ground.
Ashes. Ashes.
We all fall down.

Most hold on
according to plan,
but here's no harvest—
there are too few hands,
no one speaks,
no one understands,

and summer's wrung-out
every sound.
Ashes. Ashes.
We all fall down.

We're taught that seasons
come, then go—
each striding neatly
in its row.
The calendar
would have it so.

Yet these hang on,
through swell and heave,
to branches stripped
of burning leaves—
raw rubies dangling
till they freeze

to brown beneath
the early snow.
Defiant, still,
they will not go,
they're hollowed into
pendent ghosts

as gangs of grackles
peck their skin
in search of what
ferments within,
and frost and thaw
keep leathering

the stubborn rinds.
Black bells, unrung,
or dirty paper
lanterns slung
to shadow by
the setting sun—

they fade into
what can't be found,
dark jewels
of my eyes uncrowned.
Ashes. Ashes.
We all fall down.

  Cotillion, (Acrylic with Fabric)

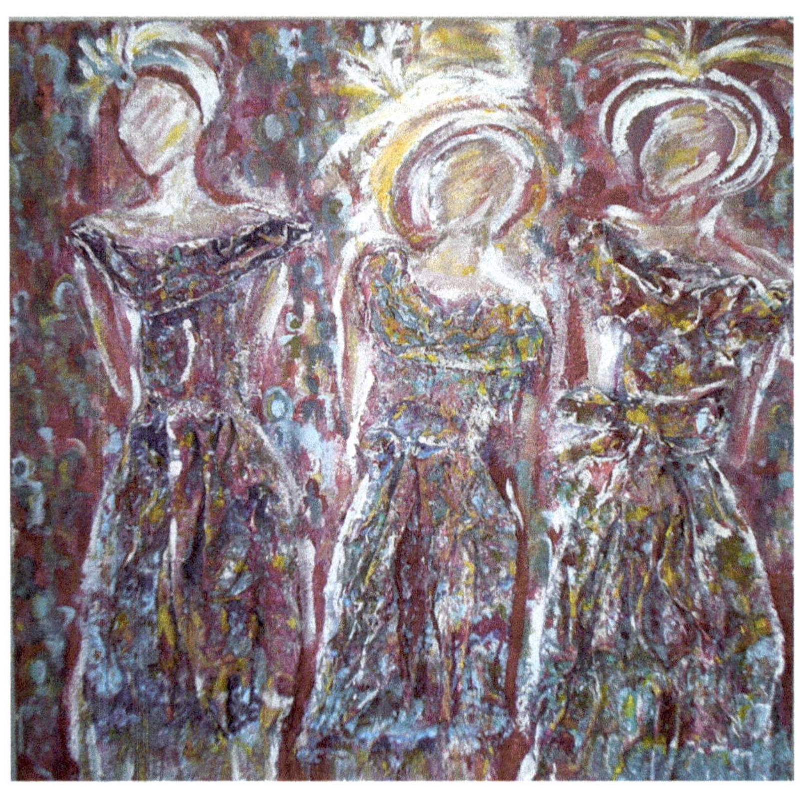

J.D. SCRIMGEOUR

Book Review: *The Queen of Queens* by Jennfer Martelli
(Bordighera Press, 2022.)

What does it mean to become a pearl? There's a hard beauty. There is also a relinquishing of the fleshiness of the oyster, the desires of appetite. A pearl is the only gemstone to come from a living creature.

The pearl is the central image in Jennifer Martelli's new collection, *The Queen of Queens.* Strands of them float across the book's cover, like waves. They are alluded to in two of the three epigraphs, and the listicle that opens and frames the collection is titled "16 Reasons I Became a Gray Pearl." "1. I grew tired of being a grain of irritation in the world's soft palate," the poem begins (13).

Pearls, of course, while beautiful, and hard, can be harvested, and, as another line in the first poem reminds us, "drilled and strung on a gold chain." Alive no longer, they become ornamental, a thing of value. Martelli's disturbing ending to her prose poem, "The Angels of Hanover Street," echos this idea. In the poem, the narrator has been discussing a sex scene in *The Godfather* with three (presumably Italian American) female friends while having dinner in the Boston's Italian neighborhood. "I love it here, in the oldest part of the city: the sticky sweet treats, the lights lit all year, the little girl-tinsel-angels dangling from hooks" (53).

In her previous book, *My Tarantella,* Martelli juxtaposes the 1964 murder of Kitty Genovese with her own upbringing as a girl in an Italian-American household and the treatment of Hillary Clinton during the 2016 presidential race. These moments were linked, she felt, in that women were not being listened to. In *The Queen of Queens,* Martilli continues to excavate her–and our–gendered American past by focusing on her college years, and specifically 1984, the year that Geraldine Ferraro–an Italian American woman– ran for vice president on the ticket with Walter Mondale. She mixes poems about Ferraro with poems about the speaker's life from that period, often incorporating female cultural touchstones, such as *Flashdance* star Jennifer Beals and Madonna, the queen of 1980s pop.

111

Martelli's book suggests that, for a young woman of that era, the unfulfilled desire to be heard was transmuted into other desires, particularly drugs and sex. "In the year of Ferraro, I loved my drugs, my runic-ludes,/ loved to dance under those mirror balls," Drugs spoke to her: *"you are heard,* they said: they said, *you are beautiful"* ("Oracular" 20).

The final reason for becoming a gray pearl in the opening poem is "16. Wanted to be dropped in a glass of red vinegar to see if I was pure enough to dissolve. I wanted to dissolve," and the book explores that desire for purity, the power of abstention. There is the theme of giving up things—drugs, meat—in order to live. But this relinquishing (the title of one of her poems) is not simply to stay alive. It's an active relinquishing, done so as not to give in. It is resistance. It is political. *"You are unable to avoid what you wish to"* says the strega who reads the speaker's palm in "Agrodolce" (27). The speaker of Martelli's poems must confront, must be confrontational, must say no as part of saying yes.

The poem "Relinquishing" ends, "The oyster, pried open for its hard/ comforting spit, looks clitoral; the salty, faceless meat" (25). It's a stunning last line, and it reminds us that the best images don't provide answers, but nudge, imply. Here, there's a suggestion that sex can make one "faceless," and, perhaps, unheard and unseen.

In contrast to this active abstention is the aunt in the prose poem "Aunt Olga Argenzio." This pathetic aunt may be the ghost who haunts this book. Somewhat locked away in the top floor of a family house, having to go down a floor into a brother's apartment to bathe, she seems a stunted creature. By memorializing the aunt, Martelli respects and preserves her life, but that life hasn't raised her consciousness; she believed it was "wrong to even ask" if women should be ordained.

Still, is to relinquish necessarily to reject? "I love it here" Martelli writes about Boston's Italian North End, and she has kept her Boston— actually Revere (Re-vee-ah)—accent. Martelli clearly rejects the conservative patriarchal Catholicism of her upbringing, yet, as she said in a conversation with me, *The Queen of Queens* is a "superstitious" book. It is from the Catholic Church, but not of it. It uses Catholic imagery, but rewrites it into its private symbology.

The book seems to identify with the "Strega" (Italian for "witch"). In a poem with that title, the speaker says "A woman/ waits in the field that grows/ along my diaphragm. She holds a yellow/ snake with pearly pink eyes." Later in the poem, the speaker declares, "I'll own what's there" (24), an assertion of taking control. "Madonna, 1984, Triptych," three sonnets of slant-rhymed couplets, begins with the young speaker stealing items from her parents' bedroom ("a tortoiseshell cup… rosaries") reminiscent of the idea of taking someone's items to take their power. The poem then moves to a dreamscape, and ends with the image of Madonna from her early MTV videos, dragging a crucifix across a room (55-56).

The secrets of this world will unlock themselves through image, both familial and communal. Still, we need to unlock language to get to them, so we have poems like "He is My Man   He is My Tomato" in which lines alternate in different columns, one column commenting in various ways on patriarchal society and Italian men, the other on tomatoes, giving facts and listing types "What is an Early Girl, a Tigerella, Three Sisters?" (31). The title itself, we learn from the helpful notes in the back of the book, is a misquotation of Geraldine Ferraro during her campaign.

While it has become trite to acknowledge that language shapes us, the best poems remind us of that fact. In "Rhymes, Slant and Otherwise," Martelli riffs on Barbara Bush's vicious comment about Ferraro, "I can't say it but it rhyme with rich." The poem is a list of various possible guesses, none anything like the word Bush is clearly implying: "Amazing grace saving not one wretch// A Dutch Elm leaf-clogged drainage ditch" (48). In doing so, it reminds us of possibilities, and makes us consider what about our culture brings that word to mind, and to whom.

In 1984, my sophomore year of college, at a party in the lounge of the dorm where I lived, a male student I knew grabbed the crotch of a woman who lived on my floor. I only heard about the incident, though I may have been at the party at the time. She was distraught. He was drunk. What happened to him? How was he punished? I don't recall. What happened to her?

I know that this story has stayed with me, perhaps because that male student's act seemed both unsurprising (I could imagine others I knew doing such a thing) and completely alien—why would he do this thing that I would never do? Martelli's book makes me not only revisit my questions, but focus more on that woman, and the women at that party, and how they processed this assault in light of the culture. It also makes me see how that time in which she and I came of age leading into our country's current social and political climate.

Reading *The Queen of Queens* now, in the immediate aftermath of the Supreme Court's denial of the reproductive rights, three of the judges appointed by the "pussy-grabber" in chief, is to feel the weight and omnipresence of patriarchy and patriarchal religious oppression. Martelli's narrator, in fact, identifies that seminal year, 1984, as a year she has an abortion ("When Was My Anger Conceived?" 58). But rather than despair by believing the (untrue) cliché that history never changes, I am fortified by the reminder that the struggle is long. Martelli dedicates the book to Geraldine Ferraro, first woman nominated to be VP from a major party. The title, The *Queen of Queens*, actually comes from Mario Cuomo's nomination speech for Ferraro ("the proud boast of the Empire State/the first lady of the Big Apple/ the Queen of Queens"). But the book also is dedicated to Kamala Harris, someone who was able to accomplish what Ferraro could not.

Martelli's poems implicitly, and sometime explicitly, speak to our current particular situation. This book is valuable for that reason alone, but a writer as brilliant with detail as Martelli—and as superstitious—knows there are deeper, more elemental truths that a poem can bring to the surface. I'll leave you with two sentences from "Aunt Olga Argenzio," describing a detail from the aunt's attic room:

> She kept her old doll on the twin bed and a box of pop-a-beads on a small bureau by the gable window. I would make necklaces over and over by sticking the plastic knobbed end into the hole of the other bead just for the satisfaction of pulling them apart, for the pop of air sucking out. When I grew older, I remembered this and how it was like sex and how it was like time.

GEORGE KALOGERIS

Book Review: ***Nike Adjusting Her Sandal***
by Anastasia Vassos
(Nixes Mate Books, 2021.)

Listen to how Anastasia Vassos recasts Cavafy in the precisely-measured, spare intensities of her own desire-haunted voice in the poem, "Being Middle Aged Back Then:"

> I look for our bench....

> I think it was this one.
> I remember how we sat here
> in the beginning
> trying to resist each other.
> How we tried to end it
> and couldn't.

These lines follow on the heels of a careful description of a walk along the Charles River Esplanade, but it's only when the speaker gets to a particular bench ("I think it was this one") that each line break registers the gathering force of latent, overwhelming emotion. As with so many of Cavafy's erotic poems, it is desire recollected over time that surges up into poetry, as if preserved in the eternal amber of congealed passion and plain-spoken exactitude. The final lines, "How we tried to end it / and couldn't" echo back the opening lines as in a perfect mirror image of suspended longing: "I could have forgotten / but didn't."

And here, in a very different register, are Vassos' beautifully moving lines of traditional lamentation:

> This bitter-ash season of your death,
> when we lit yellow candles that burned long and bright
> little chevrons of pain pointing to heaven,
> the air close, the heart closed.

The tips of the candles, "little chevrons of pain", a yellow flock of anguished feelings forever tethered to their black wicks, illuminating only "this bitter-ash season of your death." The term "close" coming right up close against the heart-stopping termination of "closed," and closure attained if only in the ritual lines of such starkly lyrical, eloquent mourning.

Between the demands of the erotic and the dearness of the familial, between the two distinctly different forms of love, in Greek, Eros and Agape, the triumph of *Nike Adjusting Her Sandal* is manifest in the poise of the poems, as ready for lyric flight as they are prepared for our earth-bound human condition. As such, the famous classical sculpture of Nike adorning the book's magnificent cover is a signal to the reader about what the poems are up to. Like the utterly translucent, wind-swept robes of the goddess, Vassos' poems are models of sensuality and clarity, and the ordinary action of strapping on a sandal is exactly the kind of homely but sculpted detail this poet seizes upon with great incisiveness.

The classical form of the female figure is also present in the poems and semi-translations that are devoted to Sappho. The great ancient lyric poet, along with the poet's parents, is a guiding voice throughout this book. In "Sappho in Translation," Vassos, a Greek-American, takes issue with Anne Carson's renowned re-castings of the ancient Greek:

> *I shall kiss*
> becomes
> *I shall love*
> according to the translator
> who thinks she knows
> better than Sappho.
>
> I prefer the bitter
> weapon of kissing—
> the mouth the charged
> organ of love's longing.

Note the line break between "who thinks she knows / better than Sappho" and the line break between "the mouth the charged / organ of love's longing." This is a gutsy poem of careful counterbalancing and passionate recalibrations, taking on Carson's appropriations (whether appropriate or not) while at the same time reminding the reader that Sappho's power is in her all too human vulnerability to Eros—the "weapon" of kissing can be turned back on the mouth of the poet, too. The "organ of love's longing" is followed by a period. Longing is never satisfied in Sappho—desire is always for what one does not have. Vassos has versified this sexual dilemma with acute feeling and critical understanding.

In the very moving "Prodigal Daughter," Vassos remembers a telephone call with her father, and how, in her college years, that summer when she was "memorizing Yeats," she rejected her father's Greek Orthodox beliefs. It was only later (we learn from other poems that he has died) that Vassos hears from her mother how, after hanging up the phone, her father had "faltered into the chair" and wept. The poem ends:

> I had been thinking
> about Petrarchan sonnets
> and that I had run out of cigarettes.

The off rhyme of "sonnets" and "cigarettes" enacts the haughty cleverness of the rebellious young writer, even as it reinforces the commitment to poetry—but not without acknowledging how far "Petrarchan sonnets" are from the household vernacular of her familial poetry, and "run out" is both limitation and the need for atonement.

At times Vassos' gift for concrete detail is fused with an equally attractive trust in evocative imagery. "In Prague" becomes an intimate, almost surreal, conjunction of outer garment and inner perception:

> I wore the tie-dyed
> shirt you like: the color
> of clouds at midnight.
>
> Later, in our room overlooking
> the black stone clock tower
> the moon shifted under my skin.

What's sublime here is the way that shifting phases of the moon is felt as a sensation articulated beneath the poet's skin, and as a perfect chime to the color of the tie-dyed shirt ("the color of clouds at midnight") and "the black stone clock tower." Midnight, the moon, the gift from someone who may or may not be a lover…. The reimagined memory of the city of Prague, at night, indelible.

Perhaps the deepest pull of desire in this book of acute lyrical longing is for the beloved dead. Listen to the intricate way that Vassos feels her way through the dark maze of loss, "syllable by syllable," her lines extending across "the middle distance" to the "porous borders" of the primordial, awesome presence of *Moira,* fate. The incantatory power of "I Will Forgive" is liturgical in its ancient rhythms, and entirely modern in its bitter resistance to conventional consolation:

> …I remember,
> as you could not, your words before you left us
> for those porous borders. Remember?
> How you made us learn prayers in ancient Greek?
> Syllable by syllable. We clenched our teeth to God.
> We gave him a name. Say *maker.* Say *middle distance.*
> Cold shudder in my ear. Sense could not be made.
> Autumn, unleafing then, the stinging time of year.
> If you get another chance, please name me Moira.
> For *bitter.* For *fate.*

In asking, praying, that she be renamed "Fate" in another life, which is the writing life, this remarkable poet realizes her calling. "I race through the dark, speaking in tongues."

GRACE BAUER

Book Review: *The Book of Jane* by Jennifer Habel
(University of Iowa Press, 2020)

Winner of the 2020 Iowa Poetry Prize, Jennifer Habel's *The Book of Jane* is a thought- provoking collection of what I might call "feminist poetry." I might also call it a "concept book," of largely "experimental" and sometimes "ekphrastic" poetry. None of these labels quite sums up the many-layered complexities of this book.

The Jane of the title is the sidekick of Dick—those characters from childhood readers we meet in this book's epigraph:

> Dick said, "I see it.
> I see the big ball."
>
> Jane said, "Oh, Dick.
> I want the little ball.
> Find the little ball.

Eighteen "Jane" poems are woven throughout the book: "Jane And The Relative Adverb," "Jane In The Guest Room," "A Guide To Jane's Office," "Jane In The Interlude," "Jane's Shame," "Jane's Souvenirs," etc. Several poems locate us in Jane's kitchen, where she encounters "Examples" of The Interrogative, The Declarative, and The Imperative—all list poems that suggest repetition and confinement. We also see "Jane's Desk," a decorative piece of furniture "at which she / did not write."

In "Jane And The Escapes," she reads the story of an enterprising octopus that managed to slip out of its tank in an aquarium, down a drainpipe, back into the sea, while another octopus stayed put. She also reads to her daughter about "a donkey that becomes a rock," but "Don't worry," we're assured in a deadpan statement, "Jane stays Jane." The poem is written in discreet lines disjointed by white space:

> How is Jane? She's Jane."

And later:

> Where is Jane going? She'll be right back.
> What is she doing? She'll be right back.

In "Jane In The Passenger Seat" we eavesdrop on a conversation between a mother and her daughter, who is referred to as "the backseat," while the driver (presumably the father) remains silent throughout. ("You'll have to / ask Dad that, Jane answers. The backseat does not / ask Dad that."). The implication is that it's the mother's job to deal with a whiney child while Dad is in control behind the wheel. After all, the poem tells us, "The passenger's job is to help." In this poem, and others, Jane's role as a mother (to daughters) is referenced; other poems suggest Jane's fraught relationship with her own mother ("except when did Jane ever have her mother").

Interspersed with the recurring adventures of Jane, are poems focused on a variety of women trying to live creative lives. Many of these poems are composed of language gleaned from other sources. "Seven Students" is a collage of quotes from *Paris Review* interviews of well-known fiction writers. Several poems ("The Pedestal," "The Concept of Service" and "The Ballet Master") are comprised of quotations from George Balanchine and several of "his" dancers, who he compares to horses, nuns, and sweet wine, before concluding that "old dancers / they should just go away / and die." The complication in these ballet poems is that the dancers themselves buy in, perhaps having no choice, to Balanchine's notion that their role is to be molded and their work a kind of "service" to his vision of what dance can be. How else to *be* a ballerina, to make the art they desire to make? Who, indeed, can tell the dancers from the (choreographer's) dance?

The various dilemmas of being a woman artist culminate in "Matisse's Great-Granddaughter, or Jane and The Long Way." This last and longest poem in the book is written in 38 numbered sections—each of them but the last numbered "1," and many of them opening with "I begin again," as if the speaker must keep trying, over and over, to get this story started. Sophie Matisse, like Jane, tries to find her own way as an artist. The fame of Sophie's surname is a challenge, as is Jane's near anonymity. Sophie makes her mark, we might say, by recreating well-known works of art by men but removing "all living figures" (often women) from the originals. On one hand this renders more women invisible—literally erasing them from the picture; on the other hand, it defies the statement of art critic John Berger: "Men act. Women appear."

The poem incorporates details of Sophie's autobiography, which suggest the challenges she faces are nothing new. Henri Matisse's mother, Anna, painted china; his daughter, Marguerite, also tried her hand at painting, but mainly devoted her life to serving her father. Sophie's grandmother, Teeny Duchamp, was first married to Pierre Matisse (Henri's son and a well-known art dealer) and then to the influential Marcel Duchamp. Teeny once had a show at the Jeu de Paume where she displayed "the prints she made of famous men's palms." Habel (and her alter ego Jane) seems to be mining this story for clues on how to proceed in her/their own creative life. In the final section of the poem (38), Habel riffs off the old Virginia Slims slogan, proclaiming "I've come the long way," which circles us back to the title—to Sophie Matisse and Jane, who gets the last line in the poem, and the book: "Oh there you are, Jane, she says."

Habel provides no easy answers to the many questions she poses in this collection. She contemplates "absent presences and present absences," discoursing "upon freedom, authority, transcendence, and female subjectivity," in highly inventive poems that rise above polemic. I suspect many women readers—especially those who are also writers or artists—will see part of themselves in Jane, or Jane as part of themselves.

Virginia Woolfe told us nearly a century ago that "for most of history, Anonymous was a woman." We may have come a long way, baby, but while fewer women writers are anonymous (no longer, we might say, *Jane Doe*), many may still sometimes feel like *plain Janes*, the less lauded sidekicks to the Dick's who rule the literary world. In this compelling collection, Jennifer Habel puts this dilemma front and center. Reader, she nails it.

STEVEN RIEL

Book Review: *The Book of Anna* by Joy Ladin
(EOAGH Books)

Never before have I quailed when reviewing a book for fear of not doing its excellence justice. Joy Ladin's *The Book of Anna* is such a powerful and skillfully wrought work of art, it has been decades since I been so transported, both intellectually and viscerally, by a book (not since Woolf's *To the Lighthouse,* in fact). In the first two sentences of this volume-length composition, the protagonist/speaker Anna Asher declares, "Today I decided to write great poetry. Or die trying." To my mind, the author herself accomplishes the "absurd" goal her imagined character audaciously trumpets. As the book's title implies, the goal is also to pen a religious (albeit unconventionally so) text, to aim for prophecy. This re-release of *The Book of Anna* in a second edition, with a new introduction that reveals the backstory of its creation, provides an opportunity to consider it from an expanded perspective now that its author has transitioned from Jay Ladin to Joy Ladin and can comment on the role that the telling of Anna's story played in that process.

The fugue-like complexity of the book's patterning (and the naturalness of that design) astounds me, as Ladin's hybrid text switches between fictional poems and diary entries, while alternately referring to biblical stories and German philosophy, and jumping between the imagined past and present of Anna's life. Although the patterning is different from that fashioned within that Hall of Mirrors that is *The Canterbury Tales,* the twisting explorations of logic and the echoes (both linear and layered) orchestrated by Ladin are equally as illuminating and satisfying as Chaucer's.

For example, consider how she employs a single word like "crack" to link and uncover truths in both the biblical story of Judah's daughter-in-law Tamar and Anna's sexual abuse by a German officer in a concentration camp. Ladin explores the syntactic, dramatic, and sonic possibilities almost obsessively, from the crack of Judah's staff hitting something hard, to a ceiling crack that leads to a mention of a crack in Heaven. The accretion of power that results from repetition (and the variation within it) gets heightened by a surrounding field of echoing short "a" sounds (rags, staff, strap, fat, slap, fact), often amplified because they show up in the words that end lines. Eventually, the narrative baton carried forward by the word "crack" gets handed off to the word "crash"—another monosyllable that lends itself to the sort of dramatic surprises Laden adeptly exploits. Later, an even more devastating interrogation of the word "designated" propels this tale of a concentration camp survivor. Eventually we discover, however, we have not heard the last "crack": it reappears much later in the book as a sound that occurs during one of the most dramatic moments in Anna's story.

There's a sense of inevitability in many of the narrative's revelations, as if everything before led to any particular unveiling. The prefigurements fit into their introductory settings so naturally that we barely notice them, until—blam!—we're left facing an unbearable atrocity or a dark joke lurking behind what we've been unsuspectingly following. (I'm avoiding spoilers.) In one section, individual words that the reader doesn't realize originate from an external quotation are first stitched into the poem's fabric, until we are presented with the full quote. Ladin successfully avoids making such set-ups feel heavy-handed. When the text interrogates a word or phrase, wringing out almost every possible drop of relevant information, almost always the effect seems organic and unforced.

One of the most compelling elements of this book is the mostly unuttered but skillfully suggested set of understandings shared between Anna and her neighbor, Suzanne Wischnauer, who lives in the same Prague apartment building, also survived the camps, and is "old enough to be my [i.e., Anna's] mother." The ironic and often comic interchanges between the two women, and Anna's thoughts about Suzanne, provide a vehicle for introducing us to Anna in the book's opening pages. We come to understand their relationship as different from but related to an even more central part of Anna's story: her relationship with her concert-pianist mother, who treated Anna with disappointment, disapproval, and some degree of negligence. Other mother figures (the farmer's wife who hides young Anna from the Nazis, older women in the camp who protect and nurture her during their imprisonment) and even Mother Nature and Planet Earth reveal the limitations and possibilities of this prime human relationship. As Anna grapples with what mothering can and cannot be, she tries to understand herself and the traumas she has experienced, all the while laboring to position her own artistic talents within the context of her mother's fame, and to build an adult self-concept that allows for self-respect if not self-love. Along the way, Anna herself takes on nurturing roles, as when she nurses Suzanne through an illness and initiates another neighbor, a 17-year-old boy, into adult sexual experience.

In this new edition's introduction, significantly titled "Anna and Me," we learn that the process of imagining Anna's intellectual, spiritual, and emotional journey allowed Ladin both to continue to mask the unconventional self that she, as "a closeted trans person," was hiding, and to provide her as author with a private arena for working out the stakes and means of a way forward in her personal life. Learning from Anna's story as she created it, Ladin "began to understand… that my need to feel alive was driving me toward ending my life as a man," but she eventually chose to bring about such closure not by suicide but by beginning to live as a trans person. This retrospective information about the author's experience of writing the book enables us to recognize yet another subtext: momentary gestures towards exposing the "Joy" Ladin hidden inside of "Jay" become noticeable. For example, in this reference to biblical names like Judah and perhaps Jesus, we discern in hindsight another "J." looking for deliverance:

> …philosophies also
> …
> become one flesh; deliver
> houses and messiahs, names
> that begin with "J"…

While fundamental questions about the possibility of a God manifested or involved in human history lie at the core of this tale of one soul wrestling with the implications of the Holocaust, surely a second central theme is that of *deliverance* of an uncomfortable self whose birth and subsequent mothering are described as a disgorgement. Ultimately, this is a text of reconstruction, of remodeling a psyche in a devastated landscape of the uncherished and brutalized. Because *The Book of Anna* interrogates so artfully and fully supreme challenges to the spirit, it earns the ambitions of a title that alludes to prophetic works: one that strives to be a literary creation dialoguing so seriously with the sacred texts of Jewish tradition as not to be found wanting in their company.

MARK WALSH

Book Review: *Between the Hours*
by Barbara Siegel Carlson
(Finishing Line Press, 2022)

I've arrived at a place with my dreaming where I can wake from a fairly intense one, replay the images – the most upsetting are usually the ones that linger – mull it over for a few minutes, then realize, "Ah! That was coming from the episode of *Breaking Bad* I watched last night." Then I fall back to sleep, those images explained and forgotten, and promise to watch more sitcoms before hitting the sack. But what's not explained, perhaps what can never be explained, is the curious way the unconscious mind reassembles those impressions in the way it does. Is it to shock, or soothe us in the middle of the night? Are dreams a steam valve or an alarm bell? And most interestingly, what is our connection to the life we live while sleeping? This is the rich territory that Barbara Siegel Carlson's new chapbook *Between the Hours* explores.

The twenty-two compact poems that make up this collection were written during the first few months of the pandemic, in a burst of creativity focused on questions about the joined mysteries of time, sleep, and dreaming. These spare poems carry significant emotional weight, offering the reader wonderful departure points to think about the ways in which our minds utilize time while our bodies are recharging. The result is a thought-provoking cycle by a poet at the top of her game.

With each poem Siegel Carlson embraces the unanswerable messages of dreams, the collage images that can scare us, or comfort us – sometimes doing both. This can be disconcerting, but Siegel Carlson never loses sight of overarching wonder, encouraging the reader to welcome and walk with these mysteries: "...others I recognize from another / unlived life. Sometimes I don't know / which world we belong to / without any borders of walls, / so clear is the dream." The fusion of disorientation and belonging shine through each line, and remind the reader that these enigmas are part of us. To deny a dream is to deny who you are.

The poems in *Between the Hours* ring with strange distance, like the fading echo of a song with a familiar melody whose lyrics are just beyond grasp. This sentiment is stated beautifully in the short poem, "The Lost Hour" :

> Maybe it's searching, calling to return, deciding who will
> disappear into it. And where does it go as it takes us
> into its clear arms?

The quicksilver quality in her lines invites each reader to explore time themselves.

There is also much to celebrate in the technique Siegel Carlson applies in this collection, my favorite being the way she loops language back on itself. A prime example of this is how "come in and be silent,"the final line of "Open the Book to Any Page," reaches back to the opening lines of "After the Words," a poem that appears two pages earlier: "I live in the silent things, the stillness / of rooms after the light has left." This reverse segue reveals how images and ideas suffuse within the poet, and provides delightful modulations of the collection's main themes.

If the pandemic brought Siegel Carlson into a meditation of time, sleep, and dreaming, it also brought her – as it did all of us – into the grief over the loss of loved ones. Her remembrance for Massachusetts poets and partners, Faye George and Winston Bolton, who died in 2020 within a week of each other, is expressed in the poignant elegy "Amid Such Breath." In that poem, she delivers a potent dose of grief squeezed into the lines, "There aren't enough / body bags for all our breath."

Between the Hours is a departure from her previous collection, Once in Every Language, itself a stunning book with a scope broad enough to range from personal loss to strangers who occupy foreign landscapes. While the dream songs of her current chapbook work in a narrower field, these poems are no less compelling.

JOSÉ ENRIQUE MEDINA

Book Review: *Far Cry* by **Tom Daley**
(Ethel Zine & Micro Press, 2022, hand-sewn chapbook)

A poet friend introduced me to Tom Daley's *Far Cry,* a chapbook in response to the death of a close gay friend with whom the author had become estranged. Because I've lived through my own painful breakup with my best gay friend, I was both excited and afraid to read these poems, wondering what dust would stir, from 30-year old wounds. I'm glad to say I survived the reading, thrived in the experience, and find myself a little sadder, a little wiser, for the effort.

Big Picture

Daley does Herculean work in terms of concentration and focus. In the era of 8-second TikTok videos and short attention spans, it's rare to find a poetry book that a) stays on subject b) addresses the same audience consistently c) unfolds and complicates a single story line and d) is written almost exclusively in the same poetic form (in this case couplets). The use of couplets is particularly effective, lulling me into the sense that I am reading, not separate poems, but one single, expanding, breathing and changing poem. The effect is not unlike reading a short novel with the satisfaction that a full story arc provides.

Even though I praise Daley's consistency, in the middle of the book, for two of the 22 poems, he drops the couplets, employing random-sized stanzas in "Just As" and tercets in "Cards and Letters." The change in form is like discovering that my long-time lover is kissing me differently. Why is he kissing me differently? Is his style of kissing changing because he's cheating and kissing someone else? Then, just as suddenly, Daley sweeps me off my feet again, and we are (figuratively) reengaged in his seductive and reassuring couplet-kissing, and my faith in his ability to transport me is restored.

Is this departure from form a misstep on Daley's part? I don't think so. In the same way that you appreciate the still reflection of a pool more after you break it into pieces and watch as clarity slowly returns, I appreciate the beauty of his poetry's consistency more after having lost it for a moment. In a book about loss and death, this produces a particularly haunting effect, like experiencing a small death. I keep returning to that spot, wondering what happened, appreciating the return to balance.

Nitty-Gritty

There are too many good lines in this collection to quote them all, so instead I will focus on a few of my favorites. For me, the whole impetus behind this book appears to be localized in these verses from the poem "Death Is the Only": "I can hardly avoid cranking / death open to permit // the ferocity of your predicaments / to tattle me upright." Strunk & White call adverbs the "leeches" of the English language, but here, Daley uses an adverb to an exquisite effect. The line wouldn't work if he'd written, "I can't avoid" or "I can almost avoid." The word "hardly" is spooky, making us consider its many meanings, including "with pain or difficulty."

On some level, the speaker is telling us he could avoid cranking death open, but chooses not to, which makes it even more frightening. And what a beautiful image: to crank death open like a window, and look inside. The "ferocity of your predicaments" (the friend's sudden and unexpected death) forces the speaker to "tattle" on himself and reveal secrets. I also enjoy the word "upright," which reminds me of a parent telling the child, "Sit upright." The image of a crooked spine straightening out is a great metaphor for the speaker fortifying himself to reveal painful truths. Another example of Daley's great word choices: the speaker says he'll "permit" the awful reality of the friend's death to enter him (he's not cranking death open, he's cranking himself open). This is one of the most vulnerable and, at the same time, empowering moments in the book, a crystallization of the poet's will to create.

I enjoy the escalation of the poems, the sense that the story has a destination. The first half of the book presents beautiful and hardline dichotomies ("Your dear and dangerous mouth," "your thumb // green with covetousness / and love," and "your cleverly / marvelous yet querulous heart"). Over and over, the speaker shows why he feels ambivalent toward his friend. However, in the second half of the book, these mixed emotions amplify into unanswered questions that disturb the speaker into acts of expression and self-doubt ("How could I have soured // so, when the record / logs so dulcet?" and "Was it better then // that I fractured / our fixture with silent // regret, a long disavowal, / rebuffing your overtures // with thin excuses…?")

In the same way that lines between who's right and who's wrong are blurred, the lines between the living and the dead are effaced in the second half of the book, raising the stakes, binding fates together. The deeper the speaker thinks, the more he realizes he's sharing the same predicaments with his deceased friend ("Over us both // the white and clamoring moon, / dividing its spell from its curse" and "Soon, / all of the spectacles // we relished together / will fall through the gaps // in our laps".)

In the last poem "I Send You Off with the Words of a Pop Song Looping in My Ears" (my favorite), the speaker further blurs the line between the past, the present and the future. He shifts back and forth, creating a new type of time in which the past is always now, the present never ages, and the future has always been here. It's also my favorite poem because for the first time it shows the two friends touching ("You're piggy on my back then, / both of us jubilant horseshoes // brawling backwards into the foam.") It's the one moment in the entire book where there are no ambivalent feelings. However, even in the speaker's happiest memory, he cannot escape the ambivalence of time, and all the good and bad that it does to us. Death is the one equivocation we cannot escape, and the chapbook ends with some of the best closing lines that I've read in a while:

> *Never a time like this to know*
> *that the future will find us*
> *but never let us go.*

Contributor Notes

ELLEN AUSTIN-LI's work has appeared in *Artemis, Thimble Literary Magazine, The Maine Review, Pine Mountain Sand & Gravel, Rust + Moth,* and other places. A Best of the Net nominee, she's published two chapbooks with Finishing Line Press: *Firefly* and L*ockdown: Scenes from Early in the Pandemic.* She earned an MFA in Poetry at the Solstice Low-Residency Program. Ellen lives with her husband in a newly empty nest in Cincinnati, Ohio. Find her work @ www.ellenaustinli.me.

GRACE BAUER has published six books of poems--most recently *Unholy Heart: New and Selected Poems.* She is also the co-editor of the anthology *Nasty Women Poets: An Unapologetic Anthology of Subversive Verse.* Her poems, essays, stories, and reviews have appeared in numerous anthologies and journals.

LAUREL BENJAMIN is a native of the San Francisco Bay Area, where she invented a secret language with her brother. Her work appears in *Lily Poetry Review, Burningword, Eunoia, Fourth River, South Florida Poetry Journal,* and *Turning a Train of Thought Upside Down: An Anthology of Women's Poetry.* Affiliated with the Bay Area Women's Poetry Salon and Ekphrastic Writers, she is a reader for *Common Ground Review* and has featured in the Lily Poetry Salon.

DENISE BERGMAN is the author of five poetry books. Published in 2021, *The Shape of the Keyhole* is about a woman falsely accused and hanged for a murder. *Three Hands None* unravels assault and its aftermath. *A Woman in Pieces Crossed a Sea* dismantles the symbolism of the Statue of Liberty. *The Telling* unfolds a child refugee's lifelong secret. S*eeing Annie Sullivan* explores the early life of Helen Keller's teacher.

ACE BOGGESS is the author of six books of poetry, including *Escape Envy* (Brick Road Poetry Press, 2021), *I Have Lost the Art of Dreaming It So,* and *The Prisoners.* His writing has appeared in *Michigan Quarterly Review, Notre Dame Review, Harvard Review, Mid-American Review,* and other journals. An ex-con, he lives in Charleston, West Virginia where he writes and tries to stay out of trouble.

MICHELLE BOLAND is a poet and essayist whose work has appeared in *Bellevue Literary Review, Cold Mountain Review, The Chaffey Review, Snapdragon: A Journal of Arts & Healing* and *Black Fox Literary Magazine,* among others. When she's not at work on her first collection of poems, she's often out connecting to the natural world around her home in the Santa Monica Mountains near Los Angeles.

JACK BORDNICK's sculptural and photographic imagery reflects his past and present forces and the imagination of his life's stories. They represent an evolutionary process of these ideas and how all of life's forces are interconnected, embraced, and expressed through creative art forms. His current sculptural images incorporate surrealistic, mythological, and magical imagery. They become abstractions unto themselves, and he allows them to revert to the origins from which they came.

SUSANA H. CASE is the award-winning author of eight books of poetry, most recently, *The Damage Done*, Broadstone Books, 2022 and co-editor with Margo Taft Stever of *I Wanna Be Loved by You: Poems on Marilyn Monroe*, Milk & Cake Press, 2022. Case worked several decades as a university professor and program coordinator in New York City, and she is currently a co-editor of Slapering Hol Press. For more, please go to https://www.susanahcase.com

STEVEN CRAMER's six poetry collections include *Listen* (MadHat Press, 2020), *Clangings* (Sarabande Books, 2012), and *Goodbye to the Orchard* (Sarabande Books, 2004), a Sheila Motton Prize-winner and a Massachusetts Honor Book. Published in *The Atlantic Monthly, The Paris Review, Poetry,* et al., and recipient of Massachusetts Cultural Council and NEA fellowships, he founded and currently teaches in Lesley University's Low-Residency MFA Program in Creative Writing.

CRAIG DOBSON has had poems published in *Acumen, Agenda, Butcher's Dog, Crannóg, The Dark Horse, The Frogmore Papers, Ink, Sweat and Tears, The Interpreter's House, The Literary Hatchet, The London Magazine, Magma, Neon, New Welsh Review, The North, Orbis, Pennine Platform, Poetry Ireland Review, Poetry Salzburg Review, Prole, The Rialto, Stand, Southword, THINK* and *Under the Radar.* He lives and works in the UK.

ABBIE DOLL is an eclectic mess of a person who loves exploring the beautiful intricacies of the written word. She resides in Columbus, OH and received her MFA from Lindenwood University; her work has been featured in *Cathexis Northwest Press, The Rush, OPEN: Journal of Arts & Letters (O:JA&L),* among others. Follow her @AbbieDollWrites.

MAHMOUD EL MARDI is a Sudanese visual artist and novelist who holds a Bachelor's degree in Fine Arts, from Sudan University of Science and Technology, College of Fine and Applied Arts. He is the recipient of the Cultural Village Award (Katara) in Qatar for fine art in 2022. His novel in short stories, published in Arabic, *The Secret of the Chisel,* includes the tale of a Sudanese young man abroad on a dangerous journey to Italy through illegal immigration. His novel in progress is *Lost in the Mango Orchards.* He aspires to support the translation of his novels into living language so that his voice can reach the world.

EVELYN ENFIELD was born and raised in the suburbs of Houston, Texas where she currently resides with her wife and young daughter. Her younger self would be disgusted with the former and in absolute awe of the later. She teaches high school English and holds an MFA in creative writing from Lesley University.

JUDSON EVANS is a full-time Instructor in the Liberal Arts & Sciences Department at Berklee College of Music. He is co-Editor of *FrogPond Journal* of the Haiku Society of America. He was chosen as an "Emerging Poet" by John Yau for The Academy of American Poets in 2007. His poems have appeared in *Folio, Volt, CutBank, The Sugar House Review* and *Laurel Review.* His collaborative book of poems *Chalk Song* (with poets Susan Berger-Jones & Gale Batchelder) was published by Lily Poetry Review Books in October 2021.

RENOIR GAITHER is an African American poet based in St. Paul, MN. He has published widely. His work has appeared in *Green Mountains Review, Berkeley Poetry Review, Obsidian: Literature & Arts in the African Diaspora, The Write Launch, Crab Fat,* and *The Birds We Piled Loosely.* His poem "The Alt-History of King Kong," originally published in *Speculative City,* was a finalist for the 2021 Ignyte Award for Best Speculative Poetry.

Nazhūn bint al-Qulāʿiya al-Gharnātiya was a courtesan in Granada, where she was infamous in her own time for her scandalous poetry that often discusses her body openly. Although only seven of her poems survive to the present, Arabic literary tradition regards her as one of the three great women poets from Andalusia.

SUSAN GRIMM has been published in *Sugar House Review, The Cincinnati Review,* and *Field.* Her chapbook *Almost Home* was published in 1997. In 2004, BkMk Press published *Lake Erie Blue,* a full-length collection. In 2010, she won the Copper Nickel Poetry Prize. In 2011, she won the Hayden Carruth Poetry Prize and her chapbook *Roughed Up by the Sun's Mothering Tongue* was published. In 2022, she received her third Ohio Arts Council Individual Artist Grant.

MAX HEINEGG's first book, *Good Harbor,* won the inaugural Paul Nemser Prize from Lily Poetry Press. His work has appeared in *32 Poems, The Cortland Review, Thrush, Nimrod,* and *Pangyrus,* among others. Find him on the web at www.maxheinegg.com

R. NEMO HILL is the author of a novel, *Pilgrim's Feather* (Quantuck Lane, 2002), a poem based on a story by H.P. Lovecraft, *The Strange Music of Erich Zann* (Hippocampus, 2004), and three poetry collections from Dos Madres Press, *When Men Bow Down* (2012), *In No Man's Ear* (2015) and *Magellan's Reveries* (2018). Forthcoming from Dos Madres Press is a book of prose from a decade of his Southeast Asian travel journals, *Just in Case It Isn't There.*

GERTRUDE HOWELl lived in Massachusetts for most of her life, where she and her husband, Richard, raised three children, and ran a household and small business. When she found quiet moments, she sat at the kitchen table and dashed out a verse, a line, a word. Her poems inspired by her life, her Faith, or her latest library read. Gertrude, known as Trudy to friends and family, passed away July 19, 2022 from Alzheimer's and late-stage leukemia at the age of 85. She would be'tickled pink" (as she liked to say) that her poem and her daughter Sarah's artwork are set together in this collaboration.

ANN HUDSON is the author of *The Armillary Sphere* (Ohio University Press) and a chapbook about radium, *Glow* (Next Page Press). Her poems have appeared or are forthcoming in *Beloit Poetry Journal, Orion, Crab Orchard Review, Colorado*

Review, North American Review, Spoon River Poetry Review, River Styx, SWWIM, Third Wednesday, and elsewhere. She is a senior editor for RHINO, and teaches at a Montessori school in Evanston, Illinois.

JULES JACOB's poems are featured in *Lily Poetry Review, Plume, Rust + Moth, Glass: A Journal of Poetry,* and elsewhere. She's the author of *The Glass Sponge;* a semi-finalist in The New Women's Voices Series (Finishing Line Press), and a recipient of a fellowship from the Virginia Center for the Creative Arts. Jules reads for *Lily Poetry Review* and can be found at julesjacob.com

CHRISTINE JONES lives in Orleans, MA and is the author of *Girl Without a Shirt* (Finishing Line Press, 2020) and co-editor of the anthology, *Voices Amidst the Virus: Poets Respond to the Pandemic* (Lily Poetry Review Books, 2020). Her second poetry book, *Now Calls Me Daughter,* is forthcoming in 2022 from Nixes Mate Review. She is the founder/editor-in-chief of *Poems2go* and associate editor of *Lily Poetry Review.* Her poetry can be found in numerous journals and anthologies in print and online.

GEORGE KALOGERIS's most recent book of poems is *Winthropos,* (Louisiana State University, 2021). He is also the author of *Guide to Greece* (LSU), a book of paired poems in translation, *Dialogos,* and poems based on the notebooks of Albert Camus, *Camus: Carnets.* His poems and translations have been anthologized in Joining Music with Reason, chosen by Christopher Ricks (Waywiser, 2010). He is the winner of the James Dickey Poetry Prize.

CRYSTAL C. KARLBERG is a Library Assistant at her local public library. She is also a speaker for Greater Boston PFLAG.

SARAH KILGALLON is originally from Boston, MA USA and now lives and creates in Lisbon, Portugal. Her visual and written works have appeared in Willow Creek Press Calendars, *Bark Magazine, The Ekphrastik Review, Wild Roof Journal,* and *Harvard Bookstore Anthologies.* Her work is currently displayed at Boston Children's Hospital, Salta in Lisbon, Portugal. She's dedicated to creating art that can hold and sustain emotional tension and continually strives for connection between her art and its audience.

DEBORAH LEIPZIGER is a poet, author, and advisor on sustainability. Her chapbook, *Flower Map,* was published by Finishing Line Press. Born in Brazil, Ms. Leipziger is the author of several books on sustainability. Nominated three times for a Pushcart Prize, Deborah's poems have been published in eight countries, including in *Pangyrus, Salamander,* and *Lily Poetry Review,* among other places. Her collection of poems is forthcoming from Lily Poetry Review Book in January 2023.

MIRIAM LEVINE is the author of *Saving Daylight,* her fifth collection of poetry. Another collection, *The Dark Opens,* was chosen by Mark Doty for the Autumn House Poetry Prize. Other books include *Devotion,* a memoir, *In Paterson,* a novel. Her work has appeared in *American Poetry Review, The Kenyon Review, The Paris Review,* and *Ploughshares.* Levine, a fellow of the NEA and a grantee of the Massachusetts Artists Foundation, lives in Florida and New Hampshire. For more information about her work, please go to miriamlevine.com.

KALI LIGHTFOOT lives in Salem, MA. Her poems and reviews of poetry books in journals and anthologies have been nominated twice for a Pushcart and once for Best of the Net. Her debut poetry collection, *Pelted by Flowers* published by CavanKerry Press was named a "most anticipated" for April 2021 by Lambda Literary; and a Best Dressed in March 2022, by Sundress Publications. Kali earned an MFA at Vermont College of Fine Arts; find her at kali-lightfoot. com

JULIA LISELLA's forthcoming collection, *Our Lively Kingdom,* (Bordighera Press 2022), was named a finalist for the Lauria/Frasca poetry prize. Other books include *Always* (WordTech, 2014), *Terrain* (WordTech, 2007), and a chapbook, *Love Song Hiroshima* (Finishing Line, 2004). Her poems are widely anthologized, and appear or will soon in *The Common, Ploughshares* and *Nimrod.* She teaches at Regis College and co-curates the Italian American Writers Association (IAWA) Reading Series in Boston.

LINDAANN LOSCHIAVO is a native New Yorker and Pushcart Prize nominee. She is a member of SFPA and The Dramatists Guild. Elgin Award winner "A Route Obscure and Lonely,"; "Concupiscent Consumption"; "Women Who Were Warned"; and "Messengers of the Macabre"; by Audience Askew (October 2022) are her latest poetry titles. Up next: a tombstone-heavy collection in hardcover by Beacon Books. Find her poetry as videos here: https://www.youtube.com/channel/UCHm1NZIlTZybLTFA44wwdfg

JENNIFER MARKELL's first poetry collection, *Samsara,* (Turning Point 2014) was named a "Must Read" book by the Massachusetts Book Awards. Her second collection, *Singing at High Altitude* was published by The Main Street Rag (November 2021). Jennifer's work has appeared in *The Bitter Oleander, The Cimarron Review, Consequence,* and *RHINO,* among other publications. She works as a psychotherapist, serves on the board of the New England Poetry Club, tends two gardens and three well-versed cats.

PAM MATZ earned an MFA in Writing from Bennington and later studied with Lucie Brock-Broido and Henri Cole. Her work has appeared or is forthcoming in *Memorious, Bloodroot, Painted Bride Quarterly, Quartet, Main Street Rag,* and *Guesthouse.* The poem "Hawk Held by a Woman" is from a series in which figures in medieval bestiaries speak.

MARTHA MCCOLLOUGH lives in Amherst, Massachusetts. She has an MFA in painting from Pratt Institute. Her poems have appeared or are forthcoming in QWERTY, Bear Review, Zone 3, and Tampa Review, among others. She is the author of Wolf Hat Iron Shoes (Lily Poetry Review Books, 2022).

SHELEEN MCELHINNEY is a Bucks County, Pa based poet whose work has appeared, or is forthcoming, in *Abandon Journal, West Trade Review, Midway Journal, Sepia Quarterly Review,* and others. Her debut book, *Every Little Vanishing,* was the winner of the 2021 Write Bloody Publishing book award.

JOSÉ ENRIQUE MEDINA earned his BA in English from Cornell University. He writes poems, flash fiction and short stories. His work has appeared in Best Microfiction 2019 Anthology, The Los Angeles Review, Tahoma Literary Review, and other publications. He is a Voices of Our Nation (VONA) fellow.

DAVID P. MILLER's collection, *Bend in the Stair,* was published by Lily Poetry Review Books in 2021. *Sprawled Asleep* was published by Nixes Mate Books in 2019. His poems have recently appeared in *Meat for Tea, The Poetry Porch, Muddy River Poetry Review, Boston Literary Magazine, Constellations, The American Journal of Poetry, Lily Poetry Review, Nixes Mate Review, Redheaded Stepchild,* and *I-70 Review.* He is a member of the Jamaica Pond Poets.

COLIN JEFFREY MORRIS is (re-)emerging as a poet after having spent much of his writing life as an academic scholar. He teaches history and American studies at Manhattanville College in Purchase, New York, lives in south Berkshire County, Massachusetts and was born and raised on England's Lancashire coast. His poems here are part of a sequence-in-progress on John James Audubon and his art.

DZVINIA ORLOWSKY is a Pushcart Prize poet, award-winning translator, and a founding editor of Four Way Books. She's the author of six poetry collections including Bad Harvest, named a 2019 Massachusetts Book Awards "Must Read" in poetry. Her co-translation with Ali Kinsella from the Ukrainian, *Eccentric Days of Hope and Sorrow: Selected Poems by Natalka Bilotserkivets,* was published by Lost Horse Press in 2021 and has been shortlisted for the 2022 International Griffin Poetry Prize.

TAMARA ORLOWSKY fled the Ukraine during WWII. She, her husband, and her parents emigrated to the US via Austria, where they sought refuge for a year in Castle Itter in exchange for her husband's medical services. They settled in Brunswick, Ohio, raising two daughters, Maria and Dzvinia. Years later, widowed in Norwell, Massachusetts, Tamara was blessed with four grandchildren: Tessa, Peter, Max, and Raisa. A self-taught artist, Tamara painted highly impressionistic flowers that often expressed a sense of loss.

STEVEN OSTROWSKI is a poet, fiction writer, painter, and professor of English at Central Connecticut State University. His work appears widely in literary journals, and he's published six chapbooks. Recently, Steven won the 2021 Wolfson Chapbook Prize for *Persons of Interest,* published in 2022 by Wolfson Press. He and his son Ben coauthored *Penultimate Human Constellation,* published in 2018 by Tolsun Books. Steven's first novel, *The Highway of Spirit and Bone,* is forthcoming from Lefora Books.

WILL PEWITT is a translator who teaches global literature at the University of North Florida and publishes in various genres, from poetry and fiction to history and philosophy. He is currently working on a book featuring his original translations of Arabic poetry predominantly by Andalusian women. More of his work can be found at WPewitt.com.

EMILY PRESENT is a writer from and still based in New York City. She co-founded and has been managing editor of the online literary magazine, *G*MOB* (formerly GlitterMOB) since 2014. Her book of poems, *Cherry Lime Gospel,* was published in 2020 by Bottlecap Press (featured in *NYLON* and *NYMag*). She is an MFA Candidate in Creative Writing at Stonybrook University where she is the recipient of The Martell Prize in Creative Writing.

JESSICA PURDY holds an MFA in Creative Writing from Emerson College. Her poems have appeared in many journals, including *One Art, Feral, Dream Pop, Impossible Task, Gargoyle, The Plath Poetry Project, The Ekphrastic Review, SurVision, The Wild Word,* and *Museum of Americana.* Her chapbook, *Learning the Names,* was published in 2015 by Finishing Line Press. Her books **STARLAND** and *Sleep in a Strange House* were released by Nixes Mate Books in 2017 and 2018.

REBECCA RESSL is a professional grant writer for community nonprofits and a volunteer at several local conservation organizations. Her work can be found or is forthcoming in *Sky Island Journal, Masque & Spectacle,* and *Unbroken Journal.* She lives in Madison, Wisconsin with her partner, child, rambunctious dog, very old cat, and piles of books.

PHOEBE REEVES earned her MFA in poetry at Sarah Lawrence College and now is Professor of English at the University of Cincinnati's Clermont College. Her chapbook *The Gardener and the Garden* was published by Seven Kitchens Press in 2019. Her poems have recently appeared in *The Gettysburg Review, Phoebe, Grist, Forklift OH,* and *The Chattahoochee Review.* You can find out more about her work at www.phoebereeves.com.

SUSAN RICH is the author of five poetry collections including *Gallery of Postcards* and *Maps: New and Selected Poems, Cloud Pharmacy* and *The Alchemist's Kitchen,* and co-editor of the anthology *The Strangest of Theatres,* published by the Poetry Foundation. Rich has received awards from PEN USA and the Fulbright Foundation. Recent poems have appeared in the Harvard Review, New England Review, Poetry Ireland and World Literature Today. Her sixth collection, *Blue Atlas,* is forthcoming from Red Hen Press in 2024. Susan is tenured faculty at Highline College outside of Seattle, WA. She is cofounder and director of Poets on the Coast: A Writing Retreat for Women.

STEVEN RIEL is the author of two full-length collections of poetry (*Edgemere* and *Fellow Odd Fellow*). His most recent chapbook *Postcard from P-town* was published as runner-up for the inaugural Robin Becker Chapbook Prize. His poems have appeared in several anthologies and numerous periodicals, including *The*

Minnesota Review and *International Poetry Review*. He currently serves as editor-in-chief of the Franco-American literary e-journal *Résonance.*

LAUREN SAXON is a queer, Black poet and engineer living in Portland, ME. She loves her cats, her Subaru, and spending way too much time on twitter (@ Lsax_235). Lauren is Editor of *Glass: A Journal of Poetry,* and her work is featured in *Flypaper Magazine, Empty Mirror, Homology Lit, Nimrod International Journal* and more. Her first chapbook, *You're My Favorite,* is forthcoming from Thirty West Publishing.

TINA SCHUMANN is the pushcart nominated author of *Praising the Paradox* (Red Hen), *Requiem. A Patrimony of Fugues,* winner of the Diode Editions award, and *As If* winner of the Stephen Dunn Prize. She is editor of the IPPY award winning anthology *Two-Countries: U.S. Daughters and Sons of Immigrant Parents,* (Red Hen). She is the poetry editor for Wandering Aengus Press and her work has appeared widely since 1999, including *Ascent, Cimarron Review, Michigan Quarterly Review, Nimrod, Poetry Daily, Rattle, Verse Daily* and on NPR's *The Writer's Almanac.* www.tinaschumann.com

J.D. SCRIMGEOUR's most recent poetry collection is the bilingual book, 香蕉面包/*BANANA BREAD* (Nixes Mate, 2021). He's the author of four other poetry collections, and two books of nonfiction, including AWP Award Winner, *THEMES FOR ENGLISH B.*

LAURALEE SIKORSKI is a Connecticut born, award-winning artist currently living in the Midwest. After showings in Chicago, Northwest Indiana, and Michigan, she traveled to London where she was juried into a Raw Arts Exhibition at the Candid Arts Center. Her artwork was purchased into a private collection. Sikorski's work is highly eclectic in both subject matter and medtiums used. Enjoying the Influences of Salvador Dali and Jean Michel Basquiat, her latest projects include large-scale, outdoor public sculptures and three-dimensional murals.

JANICE D. SODERLING has published hundreds of poems, flash fiction and short stories in print and online international journals. Her most recent collection is Rooms & Closets. She lives in Sweden.

ANNIE STENZEL (she/her) was born in Illinois but did not stay put. Her poems have been published in print or online journals in the U.S. and UK including *Ambit, Chestnut Review, Gargoyle, Kestrel, Nixes Mate, On the Seawall, Shot Glass Journal, Slipstream, SWWIM, The Lake,* and *Thimble.* A poetry editor for *Right Hand Pointing* and *West Trestle Review,* she now lives on unceded Ohlone land within walking distance of the San Francisco Bay.

LISA J. SULLIVAN holds an MFA in Poetry from the Solstice MFA Program, where she was a Kurt Brown Memorial Fellow. Her work has appeared in *The American Journal of Poetry, The Comstock Review, Evening Street Review,* and elsewhere.

She was the United States winner of the 2013 Ireland Poetry Project contest in conjunction with the Academy of American Poets. Lisa is the art editor of *Lily Poetry Review* and a poetry editor for *Pink Panther Magazine.*

UMM AL-KIRAM BINT AL-MU'TASIM IBN SUMADIH was a princess whose father ruled Almería. When he realized his daughter's intelligence, he gave her the same education as his sons. Later in life, when he heard of her love for a court eunuch, as-Samar, he had the eunuch murdered. Supposedly, every one of her poems is for as-Samar.

MARIA SURRICCHIO is originally from the UK and now lives near Boulder, Colorado. A life-long lover of poetry, she turned to writing in 2020 after a long marketing career. Her work has been published, and is forthcoming, in the *I-70 Review, Delta Poetry Review* and *The Dillydoun Review.* She has a BA in Modern Languages from Cambridge University.

CARINE TOPAL is the recipient of many poetry awards including the Robert G. Cohn Prose Poetry Award, The Briar Cliff Review Poetry Award, and the Palettes and Quills Chapbook Contest. Her fifth and latest collection, *In Order of Disappearance* was published by the Pacific Coast Poetry Series in January 2018. Her work has appeared in journals such as *The Iron Horse Literary Review, The Best of the Prose Poem, Greensboro Review,* and many others. She teaches poetry and memoir by the sea and in the desert of Southern California.

ANASTASIA VASSOS is a Greek American writer from Boston. She is the author of *Nike Adjusting Her Sandal* (Nixes Mate, 2021). Her chapbook *The Lesser-Known Riddle of the Sphinx* was a finalist in Two Sylvias Press 2021 Chapbook Contest. Her poems appear in *Thrush, RHINO, SWWIM, Comstock Review* and elsewhere. She is a reader for *Lily Poetry Review,* speaks three languages, and is a long-distance cyclist.

STEPHEN VINCENT is an artist, poet, and maker of books, whose work is exhibited and collected in many places including Getty Research Institute, Berkeley Art Museum, Stanford University Library, Center for The Book, and the Oliver Ranch Foundation. His poetry and combined poetry and art titles include *Walking, Walking Theory, After Language: Letters to Jack Spicer, The First 100 Days of Obama,* and *The Last 100 Days of The Presidency of Barack Obama.*

MARK WALSH is a professor of English at Massasoit Community College in Brockton, MA, where he teaches Introduction to Philosophy, Composition and British Literature. He has organized poetry events and readings in Plymouth, Quincy, and Brockton. Mark is also a writer, having stories, articles, and poems published in various newspapers and literary magazines including *The GW Review, Theaurora,* and most recently *Everyone Has a Voice.*

NANCY WHITE is the author of three poetry collections: *Sun, Moon, Salt* (winner of the Washington Prize), *Detour,* and *Ask Again Later.* Her poems have appeared in *Beloit Poetry Review, FIELD, New England Review, Ploughshares, Rhino,* and many others. She serves as editor-in-chief at The Word Works in Washington, D. C. and teaches at SUNY Adirondack in upstate NY.

FIONA WILKES is a current PhD Candidate at The University of Western Australia specializing in English & Literary Studies. A fierce feminist, her work focuses on the plights of women & queer folk of the past, present, and future.

JOHN SIBLEY WILLIAMS is the author of four award-winning poetry collections, including *The Drowning House, Scale Model of a Country at Dawn, As One Fire Consumes Another,* and *Skin Memory.* A twenty-seven-time Pushcart nominee, John is the winner of numerous awards, including the Wabash Prize for Poetry, Philip Booth Award, and Laux/Millar Prize. He serves as editor of *The Inflectionist Review* and founder of the Caesura Poetry Workshop series.

ROS ZIMMERMANN is a multi-media poet whose work unfolds words as visual images and soundscapes on the page. Recent poems appear in *Poems About Sculpture* (Random House), *Solstice: A Magazine of Diverse Voices, terrain. org, Field Guide, Let the Bucket Down, Boog City, Collaborative Poem Project: A Living Anthology,* and in Wesleyan University's *Best American Experimental Writing Online (BAX).* Other works include a creative/critical work on Rachel Blau DuPlessis, "Incomplete Closures" *(Journal of Poetics Research, JPR05), STILL MOVING,* a collaborative dance and video piece, and *Intemperate Zone,* a collaboration with artist Nancy Selvage at the Boston Sculptors Gallery (March 2019).